Carnegie Mellon University

Pittsburgh, Pennsylvania

Written by Dan Liebermann
Edited by Christina Koshzow

Additional contributions by Omid Gohari,
Christina Koshzow, Chris Mason, Joey Rahimi,
Jon Skindzier, Luke Skurman, Tim Williams

COLLEGE PROWLER

ISBN # 1-59658-023-2
ISSN # 1551-9686
© Copyright 2005 College Prowler
All Rights Reserved
Printed in the U.S.A.
www.collegeprowler.com

Special thanks to Babs Carryer, Andy Hannah, LaunchCyte, Tim O'Brien, Bob Sehlinger, Thomas Emerson, Andrew Skurman, Barbara Skurman, Bert Mann, Dave Lehman, Daniel Fayock, Chris Babyak,The Donald H. Jones Center for Entrepreneurship, Terry Slease, Jerry McGinnis, Bill Ecenberger, Idie McGinty, Kyle Russell, Jacque Zaremba, Larry Winderbaum, Paul Kelly, Roland Allen, Jon Reider, Team Evankovich, Julie Fenstermaker, Lauren Varacalli, Abu Noaman, Jason Putorti, Mark Exler, Daniel Steinmeyer, Jared Cohon, Gabriela Oates, Tri Ad Litho, David Koegler, Glen Meakem, and the CMU Bounce Back Team.

College Prowler™
5001 Baum Blvd.
Suite 456
Pittsburgh, PA 15213

Phone: (412) 697-1390, 1(800) 290-2682
Fax: (412) 697-1396, 1(800) 772-4972
E-mail: info@collegeprowler.com
Website: www.collegeprowler.com

Welcome to College Prowler™

During the writing of College Prowler's guidebooks, we felt it was critical that the information within was unbiased, and that the guides were unaffiliated with any college or university. We think it's important that our readers get honest information and a realistic impression of the student opinions on any campus—that's why if any aspect of a particular school is terrible, we (unlike a campus brochure) intend to publish that fact. While we do keep an eye out for the occasional extremist—the cheerleader or the cynic—we take pride in letting the students tell it like it is. We strive to create a book that's as representative as possible of each particular campus. Our books cover both the good and the bad, and whether the survey responses point to recurring trends or a variation in opinion, these sentiments are directly and proportionally expressed through our guides.

College Prowler guidebooks are in the hands of students throughout the entire process of their creation. Because you can't make student-written guides without the students, we have students at each campus who help write, randomly survey their peers, edit, layout, and perform accuracy checks on every book that we publish. From the very beginning, student writers gather the most up-to-date stats, facts, and inside information on their colleges. They fill each section with student quotes and summarize the findings in editorial reviews. In addition, each school receives a collection of letter grades (A through F) that reflect student opinion and help to represent contentment, prominence, or satisfaction for each of our 20 specific categories. Just as in grade school, the higher the mark the more content, more prominent, or more satisfied the students are with the particular category.

Once a book is written, additional students serve as editors and check for accuracy even more extensively. Our bounce-back team—a group of randomly selected students who have no involvement with the project—are asked to read over the material in order to help ensure that the book accurately expresses every aspect of the university and its students. This same process is applied to the 200-plus schools College Prowler currently covers. Each book is the result of endless student contributions, hundreds of pages of research and writing, and countless hours of hard work. All of this has led to the creation of a student information network that stretches across the nation to every school that we cover. It's no easy accomplishment, but it's the reason that our guides are such a great resource.

When reading our books and looking at our grades, keep in mind that every college is different and that the students who make up each school are not uniform—as a result, it is impor-tant to assess schools on a case-by-case basis. Because it's impossible to summarize an entire school with a single number or description, each book provides a dialogue, not a decision, that's made up of 20 different topics and hundreds of student quotes. In the end, we hope that this guide will serve as a valuable tool in your college selection process. Enjoy!

OMID GOHARI ◯ CHRISTINA KOSHZOW ◯ CHRIS MASON ◯ JOEY RAHIMI ◯ LUKE SKURMAN ◯
The College Prowler™ Team

CARNEGIE MELLON
Table of Contents

Introduction from the Author

When people ask me where I'm going to college, I'll sheepishly reply, "Carnegie Mellon University." It's with a look of sheer stupefaction that they nod approvingly, never having heard of the school and thinking me a fool for receiving my college education from a grocer. On the other hand, the people I talk to who are aware of the University's incredible accomplishments respond differently. Their faces light up and they energetically reply, "Really? Wow, you must be smart!" The way things are going, I might be hearing this reply much more often.

Carnegie Mellon University is growing and improving so rapidly, that its name recognition hasn't caught up with it yet. It's only in the last twenty years that the University has begun its ascent into the upper echelon of the nation's colleges, a place where it is sure to stay for some time. If one thing is happening on campus, it's growth. As the University expands its size and academic options, the school's students continue to grow with it. Carnegie Mellon is intent on molding its students into professionals, and it succeeds.

Honestly, I'd never even heard of Carnegie Mellon until it was time for my college search. It's hard to paint an accurate portrait of the school with just facts and statistics. CMU has a unique cultural dynamic that defines the University in the eyes of its students. When you have a professional University, composed of five nationally-commended colleges in fields ranging from computer science to the fine arts, you're guaranteed a certain level of intellectualism. When you have students from around the world participating in a campus environment where diversity is embraced and treasured, all wrapped in the hills of Pittsburgh Pennsylvania, you're guaranteed a certain level of perspective. Some students would even say that when you have a Carnegie Mellon degree you're guaranteed a certain level of salary.

If you're interested in CMU, you probably already know all that it can offer you in terms of academics and professionalism. Now be prepared to ask yourself a larger question. Do you want to spend the next four years of your life there? No matter how much information you know about a college, that's not an easy question to answer. Hopefully, this book can provide you with some insight into what life is really like at Carnegie Mellon University.

Daniel Lieberman, Author
Carnegie Mellon University

By the Numbers

General Information

Carnegie Mellon University
5000 Forbes Avenue
Pittsburgh, PA 15213

Control:
Private

Academic Calendar:
Semester

Religious Affiliation:
None

Founded:
1900

Website:
http://www.cmu.edu

Main Phone:
(412) 268-2000

Admissions Phone:
(412) 268-2082

Student Body

**Full-Time
Undergraduates:**
5,226

**Part-Time
Undergraduates:**
258

**Total Male
Undergraduates:**
3,299

**Total Female
Undergraduates:**
2,185

Male to Female Ratio:
60:40

Admissions

Overall Acceptance Rate:
38.12%

**Early Decision
Acceptance Rate:**
49%

Regular Acceptance Rate:
38%

Total Applicants:
14,467

Total Acceptances:
5,561

Freshman Enrollment:
1,341

**Yield (% of admitted
students who actually
enroll):**
24%

Early Decision Available?
Yes

Early Action Available?
No

Early Decision Deadline:
November 1

Early Decision Notification:
December 15

Regular Decision Deadline:
January 1

**Regular Decision
Notification:**
April 15

Must Reply-By Date:
May 1

**Common Application
Accepted?**
Yes

Supplemental Forms?
Yes

Admissions Phone:
(412) 268-2082

Admissions Email:
admissions.office@cmu.edu

Admissions Website:
www.cmu.edu/enrollment/ad-mission

SAT I or ACT Required?
Either

**SAT I Range
(25th – 75th Percentile):**
1280-1470

**SAT I Verbal Range
(25th – 75th Percentile):**
600-700

**SAT I Math Range
(25th – 75th Percentile):**
680-770

Retention Rate:
95.6%

**Top 10% of
High School Class:**
72%

Application Fee:
$60

→

Applicants placed on waiting list:
2,941

Applicants accepting a place on waiting list:
294

Students enrolled from waiting list:
180

Transfer applications received:
338

Transfer applicants offered admission:
59

Transfer applicants enrolled:
32

SAT II Requirements for:

Carnegie Institute of Technology
Architecture
Math I, Ic, or IIc, Physics or Chemistry, Writing

Humanities and Social Sciences:
Math I, Ic, or IIc, Writing, One additional test selected by applicant

Mellon College of Science
Computer Science
Industrial Administration

Math I, Ic, or IIc, Physics, Chemistry, or Biology, Writing

Information Systems:
Math I, Ic, or IIc, Writing, One additional test selected by applicant

Financial Information

Full-Time Tuition:
$31,036 per year.

$40 registration fee
per semester

Room and Board:
$8,554

Books and Supplies for class:
$910 per year

Average Need-Based Financial Aid Package:
$21,658 per year

Students Who Applied For Financial Aid:
60%

Students Who Received Aid: 51%

Financial Aid Forms Deadline: February 15

Financial Aid Phone:
(412) 268-8186

Financial Aid E-mail:
thehub@andrew.cmu.edu

Financial Aid Website:
http://www.cmu.edu/hub

Academics

The Lowdown On...
Academics

Degrees Awarded:
Bachelor
Master
Doctorate

Most Popular Areas of Study:

13% computer engineering, 12% computer science, 10% business administration and management, 7% mechanical engineering, 6% information science/studies

Undergraduate Schools:

Carnegie Institute of Technology
College of Fine Arts
College of Humanities and Social Sciences
Mellon College of Science
School of Computer Science
School of Industrial Administration

Fulltime Faculty:	**Average Course Load:**
1,000	5 courses

Faculty with Terminal Degree:
96%

AP Score Requirement
Possible credit for scores of 4 or 5

Student-to-Faculty Ratio:
10:1

IB Score Requirement
Possible credit for scores of 6 or 7

Special Degree Options

Dual-Degree Programs
Biomedical Engineering, Engineering and Public Policy, Biology and Psychology

Accelerated Master's Programs
Public Management and Policy, Information Systems, Business Administration

Intercollege Programs
Bachelor of Humanities and Arts, Bachelor of Science and Arts, Science and Humanities Scholar

Sample Academic Clubs
The Law Society, the National Society of Black Engineers, the Investment Club, the Society of Hispanic Professional Engineers, the Filmmaking Club

Four-year graduation rate:
66%

Five-year graduation rate:
78%

Six-year graduation rate:
81%

Did You Know?

"The two universities that have made the most phenomenal gains [in the last two decades] are Stanford and Carnegie Mellon."

–George Keller, author of Academic Strategy: The Management Revolution in Higher Education

Want to go to class without leaving your dorm?

Carnegie Mellon now offers a few of its courses online.

Need help on your test?

Just go inside the front door of Baker Hall. Students in the School of Humanities and Social Sciences often rub the nose of Hamerschlag's statue for good luck.

Primal Scream!

Once a semester during finals, students gather outside during the middle of the night to participate in Primal Scream—a chance to yell, eat food, and relieve stress.

What Are Units?

Carnegie Mellon assigns "unit" values instead of "credits" to each of its courses in order to represent the amount of work that is required by a particular class. One unit equals one hour of work, so a nine-unit class means that you'll have approximately nine hours of work a week. Most classes are between nine and twelve units.

Best Places to Study

Library

University Center

Students Speak Out On...
Academics

"When I got here, I thought that it would be difficult to meet with my professors if I needed help outside of class. I was pleasantly surprised to find out that the professors care a lot about their students and will stay well after class to help you with what you need. I've had a lot of professors that are all friendly and make class fun while teaching in unique and lively ways."

Q "The teachers in the art department are good. **I really respect them.** Some of the others have gotten lazy and are more interested in research than in teaching classes."

Q "The teachers at CMU are very nice. They are a**lways willing to lend a helping hand**, and the teaching assistants (TAs) are usually pretty good. There are always a few that slip by and end up teaching a subject they have no experience with, but the majority of TAs are extremely well-qualified. Some have even taught the course in previous semesters."

Q "It really depends on the subject and the teacher on a case-by-case basis. Overall, the professors are very dedicated, but **some teachers are just straight morons** and it's impossible to figure out why they teach. My physics professor didn't know the first thing about educating anyone on the subject, and I swear my English professor was a raving drunk who just pulled the entire class discussion out of his butt every Tuesday and Thursday. On the other hand, I've learned invaluable things from some very professional teachers on the subjects of video, design, and anthropology."

Q "Academics are excellent! The attention you personally get from your professors, who are the best in their field, is unbelievable. **The opportunities here are fantastic**, and you're only limited by what you can imagine."

Q "Usually, dealing with administrative stuff is extremely frustrating, but the academic experience is great if you have the right professors. There will always be a few professors that you will hate, but the ones that you grow to really enjoy **make it worthwhile**."

Q "Professors tend to be better as you get older. Unfortunately, there are a lot of teaching assistants and lower-level professors that speak in strong accents and make things difficult. I've found that **the level of knowledge is phenomenal,** but lots of professors are more interested in research than in students. It really depends on the professor."

Q "This school is excellent, academically. It is ranked in the top twenty-five universities in the country. It's the best place in the world to study robotics. It ranks in the top ten for engineering, computer science, and business. Plus, the College of Fine Arts has numerous famous alumni. In fact, the school of drama is in the top three of all theater programs in the United States and is also the oldest drama degree-granting program. **The teachers are easily accessible;** they all have office hours, and most of the classes are pretty small so that questions can be asked."

Q "Teachers and academics are awesome! If you come here, **you better be serious about learning** because you will get swept away if you aren't. Pretty much everything we do here is good. All of our sciences kick butt, and our drama and theatre programs are really exceptional, too. We are cool like that because we have both nerds and artists—it makes things interesting."

Q "The quality of education **depends on your major**, I guess. From the few classes I've taken in H&SS (Humanities and Social Sciences), I think their humanities department isn't that great. At least the introductory courses aren't the best. If you're into a technological field, then

the school is not bad. I think the computer science program is not bad at all. The teachers usually know what
they're talking about, which is unlike most other places.
Regardless, it really depends on your major."

"The professors are pretty good here; it depends on the
class. I got to know my business professor really well.
He knew all of our names (there were eighty-five of us)
within the first few weeks, and we see him everywhere. He
always stops and chats for a little while. He's also the head
of the business department. If you make an effort, **you
can really get to know your professors**, but as far as
teaching quality goes, I guess most professors are good.
Everyone has their own favorites. If you come to CMU,
just ask any upper classman and they'll tell you that the
teachers are great at what they do and are into cutting-
edge research, so they're never out of touch with what is
modern. You can't be ranked as high as CMU is without
having good professors."

The College Prowler Take On...
Academics

It often feels like CMU is just a school with brilliant students struggling to get by in a never-ending onslaught of hard work. In the rush of our academic diligence, CMU students can often forget the role our professors play in furthering our education. That said, CMU professors run the gamut from, "I'm a pioneer in my field," to "I'm teaching this class so I can do research here." One thing that can be said about all the professors though, is that they're very approachable. Professors will always find time to meet with you after class or respond to your e-mails. As a student, your relationship with your professors is largely what you make it.

The excellent academic reputation is the reason why most prospective students become interested in Carnegie Mellon in the first place. The school maintains an interesting dichotomy with its success in both its technological and artistic pursuits. Many people consider CMU's technical majors to be the most successful, and accordingly, they've received national acclaim.

The College Prowler™ Grade on
Academics: A-

A high Academics grade generally indicates that Professors are knowledgeable, accessible, and genuinely interested in their students' welfare. Other determining factors include class size, how well professors communicate, and whether or not classes are engaging.

Local Atmosphere

The Lowdown On...
Local Atmosphere

Region:
Northeast

City, State:
Pittsburgh, Pennsylvania

Setting:
Medium-Sized City

Distance from Cleveland:
2.5 hours

Points of Interest:
Carnegie Museum of Art
The Andy Warhol Museum
Heinz Hall
The Mattress Factory
Schenley Park
PNC Park, Heinz Field
Kennywood Park
Point State Park (The Point)
The Waterfront
Southside (Carson Street)
Shadyside (Walnut Street)
Squirrel Hill (Murray Avenue)
Oakland

→

Closest Shopping Malls:

The Waterfront
Monroeville Mall
Ross Park Mall

Closest Movie Theatres:

Loews at the Waterfront
300 W. Waterfront Dr
Homestead
(412) 462-6384

Cinemagic Theatre
5824 Forward Ave.
Squirrel Hill
(412) 421-7900

Cinemagic Manor Theatre
1729 Murray Ave., Squirrel Hill
Phone: (412) 422-7729

Major Sports Teams:
Steelers (football)
Pirates (baseball)
Penguins (hockey)

City Websites

www.city.pittsburgh.pa.us/
www.pittsburgh.citysearch.com
www.pittsburgh.com

Local Slang

Pop – what a Pittsburgher calls soda

Yinz/yunz – rumored to have originated from "you ones;" similar meaning as y'all

Gumband – rubber band

Red up – to clean up

5 Fun Facts about Pittsburgh:

1. In addition to being called one of America's most livable cities, Pittsburgh is also known as the City of Champions, thanks to its legendary sports teams.

2. Pittsburgh is a beer town. Home to a number of breweries, the city makes its local favorite, Iron City, right here.

3. The Mothman Prophecies, Dogma, Silence of the Lambs, The Wonder Boys, Kingpin, Night of the Living Dead, Inspector Gadget, and many more movies were all filmed here.

4. If you like new stadiums, Pittsburgh has two of them. Both The Pittsburgh Pirates and the Steelers have two brand-new, state-of-the-art facilities on the North Shore.

5. The Duquesne Incline and the Monongahela Incline are cable cars that run up the side of Mt. Washington and provide riders with a fantastic view of the city.

Famous Pittsburghers:

Dennis Miller

Michael Keaton

Andy Warhol

Perry Como

Henry Mancini

George Benson

August Wilson

Rachel Carson

Christina Aguilera

Jeff Goldblum

Mr. Rogers

Stephen Foster

Ahmad Jamal

Gene Kelly

Gertrude Stein

➜

Students Speak Out On...
Local Atmosphere

"Pitt is pretty close. There are tons of museums around campus, if you're into that kind of stuff. My favorite place to go on the weekends is the Waterfront. They've got shopping, great restaurants, and a huge movie theater."

"I don't feel like I've seen much of Pittsburgh. **It's so spread-out.** I heard the Strip District is nice"

"Although CMU is in the city of Pittsburgh, I'd say that it's on the outskirts of the city and closer to a few suburbs. We're down the street from Pitt, but since our school is on a campus and not along several streets, it's rare that you see Pitt kids up here. **Stay away from the drunk frat boys** during your freshmen week of orientation—they can get pretty rowdy, especially if you walk around with everyone from your whole dorm floor!"

"**Pittsburgh is not an exciting town.** It's a strange mix between a suburban mini-mall atmosphere and a major national city with tons of residential areas mixed up in-between. Yeah, there are tons of other universities present—U. Pitt, Chatham, Duquesne, Point Park, Robert Morris—but chances are, if you are at CMU you won't have any desire to socialize with these people anyway. Most likely, you'd prefer a quiet evening of staying in your dorm room and gaming on line with your friends. Go to a Pirates game because the stadium is sweet beyond words."

"There are lots of good theatres downtown and on campus. We've got one of the best drama programs in the world, so you want to take advantage of that as much as

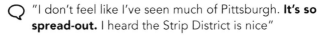

possible. **The baseball park is nice, too, and tickets are cheap.**"

Q "One thing that sucks is that **stuff tends to close really early around here.** I don't get it at all, but it's true. Besides that, we have the Steelers, the Penguins, and the Pirates not even ten minutes away by car. There are museums, a downtown, and Kennywood's roller coasters all really close. You can always find something cool to do."

Q "I like Pittsburgh. It's a nice medium-sized city. I think **it's beautiful because of the mountains and rivers**, plus I find enough to do here. We have some really great museums just down the street. If you like sports, there are the Steelers and the Pirates. The symphony is excellent, and there are some good theaters, although the best place for theater is on campus—the school of drama does around fifteen different shows a semester. We also have a big park adjoining our campus, plus with the University of Pittsburgh, Duquesne University, Chatham College, Carlow College, Robert Morris College, and some community colleges, the city is quite student-friendly."

Q "You're in the good old city of Pittsburgh. It's a good town to go to school in because you can get your work done without having to worry about seeing all of the marvelous things there are to see. Besides partying and clubbing at semi-decent nightclubs, there are some nice museums, sporting events, and shows you can catch, but it's nothing like a major metropolitan city. I'd **stay away from the Hill District**, though."

Q "The University of Pittsburgh is just down the street. There are bars and clubs down there. The guys and girls are more attractive at Pitt, but there are not many places that are open real late. Clubs and bars close around 2 a.m. unless they're after-hours clubs. **Shopping isn't all that great.** You have generic stores, but other than that, nothing exciting. There are a few interesting things to do in Pittsburgh, but options are limited."

The College Prowler Take On...
Local Atmosphere

Allegheny County may be the second most elderly county in the nation, but that doesn't make Pittsburgh any less of a college town. With U. Pitt right down the street and Duquesne and Chatham nearby, there are lots of local stores tailored to college crowds. If you like coffee shops, there's more than enough of them in the area surrounding CMU to satisfy your thirst. During the school year, you can't go wrong walking down Forbes or Fifth Avenue—chances are you'll stumble upon some concert, restaurant, party, or bar.

In addition, the residential neighborhoods of Squirrel Hill and Shadyside are a nice compliment to Oakland's college atmosphere. These nearby areas offer students some variety in upscale dining and shopping. For the adventurous student, downtown Pittsburgh has a lot to offer as long as you know where you're going. Unfortunately, however, Downtown does not offer the same youth and cultural scene as larger cities like New York or Chicago.

The College Prowler™ Grade on

Local Atmosphere: B-

A high Local Atmosphere grade indicates that the area surrounding campus is safe and scenic. Other factors include nearby attractions, proximity to other schools, and the town's attitude toward students

Safety & Security

The Lowdown On...
Safety & Security

of CMU Police:
17

CMU Police Phone:
412 268-2323 (emergencies)
412 268-6232 (non-emergencies)

Safety Services:
(RAD) Rape Defense classes
Campus Watch
Safe Walk
Shuttle/Escort Van
Emergency Phones

Health Services:
Basic medical services
On-site pharmaceuticals
STD screening
Counseling and psychological services

Health Center Hours
Monday, Tuesday, and Thursday 8 a.m.-7 p.m.
Wednesday 10 a.m.-7 p.m.
Friday 8 a.m.-5p.m.
Saturday 11 a.m.-3 p.m.

Students Speak Out On...
Safety & Security

"In my opinion, CMU's campus is really safe. We'll occasionally have conflicts but as long as you use common sense and don't walk down a shady avenue at two in the morning, you'll be fine."

"**I feel pretty safe on campus**, even walking around late at night. There are blue call boxes around campus just in case there is an emergency. Supposedly, you can see one from everywhere on campus, but I don't know who has actually tested this. This past year, I lived off campus and used the CMU escort service several times. It's a van that picks you up on campus at several locations and then drops you off at your residence. It's pretty convenient and great for leaving a friend's dorm, the library, or maybe even the cluster late at night."

"The campus has had its share of assaults—sexual or otherwise—but they are few and far between. **CMU is in a city with plenty of dark alleys to walk down**, so you have to exercise caution and judgment, but if you act somewhat appropriate, you should be safe. The police try very hard to make the socially naive student body feel comfortable in Pittsburgh. Just don't walk around in certain areas by yourself later at night. It's always a good idea to go places with friends and try to take the bus at night to areas you are unfamiliar with."

"The campus is relatively safe. The biggest problem, I think, is bike theft. Not much happens on campus other than **drunken kids being rowdy**. There is a crime report section on the CMU website, so you can check that out."

Q "The crime rate has been very low; most crimes involve **stealing bikes and unattended laptop** computers or underage drinking on campus."

Q "I think that **things are pretty safe** on CMU's campus. It's not that hard to find campus police officers walking around, no matter when. They have routine check-ups on the street as well as in the dorms. Also, they e-mail students whenever there are some events within or around the campus that may affect the campus security, so you should know better than to walk around without a preparation."

Q "It's normally good, but there are some bad incidents sometimes. I never heard of anyone who has gotten killed, but I have heard about **certain cases of attempted rape** by strangers, and one case was of an actual rape. There is a region by the school that is also not that safe which is around the University of Pittsburgh. I think as long as you hang out with a large crowd, you should always be fine."

Q "Security is pretty good at CMU, and **I feel safe walking around campus at any time of the day or night**. I usually hang out with friends till the wee hours in the night and I live on the other side of campus. I don't have any problems walking back alone. There are services though, like campus police and escort services that will pick you up from wherever you are and take you back to your room. We also have this new program called Safe Walk, where two students walk with you to wherever you need to go. So, I think security and safety is well taken care of on campus. Honestly, there have been a few incidents in the past with attempted assaults, but the University quickly responded by having more campus police all around."

Q "Pittsburgh is a city that makes security a big issue. The **campus police are fairly active**; I see them walking or driving around just about every day. I would say that the biggest issue here is sexual assault. There have been a few—two or three over the course of the year—security bulletins posted about young females being attacked by people because they were walking alone late at night."

Q "CMU has an interesting security situation. Basically, CMU has its own police force. **Campus police are always around,** especially at night and frequently during the day. I feel very safe whenever I walk to and from class. I mean, it's not a very large campus, so I don't think you have too much to worry about with that. However, I have noticed that there were a lot of cases of assault—probably four to five—and one case of a mugging, but the campus police handle it very well. They post you with up-to-date information on where to be careful and places to avoid; I wouldn't sweat it."

Q "Well, **there were a few attempted robberies, but they all failed.** As a result, however, they're trying to add more emergency phones around; there's not enough right now. Also, there's a group that is usually active called Safe Walk, and they will send two escorts to walk you at night. Also, there were very few safety breaches within the dorm."

The College Prowler Take On...
Safety & Security

Students are in agreement that, although there is crime on and around campus, they feel secure and are not too concerned about their safety. Campus initiatives like SafeWalk and the escort van service have really helped students to feel safer. Two police cars and one supervisor patrol the campus 24 hours a day. Dorm security, however, is very lax. Quickly flashing your ID at the entrance to any dorm is enough to get you, all your friends, and that garbage bag filled with beer that you're holding into the building. Recent efforts to monitor who comes in and out of the dorms have been largely unsuccessful due to the fact that the desk attendant position is student-run. Complaints about bikes are well-founded too. It is very common to see the dismembered handle-bars and spokes of bikes that have been destroyed still chained to the rack. Whoever has a passion for destroying these bikes is still pretty much a mystery.

The CMU police should also be commended for maintaining a highly visible presence and giving the campus such a safe feel. Because of the campus's polished professional atmosphere, it's easy to forget that walking just a few blocks off campus could possibly put you in a much worse area. However, while there aren't many instances of crime by students, it goes without saying that valuables (laptops) left unprotected or unlocked in a campus locker run a high risk of being stolen.

B+

The College Prowler™ Grade on

Safety & Security: B+

A high grade in Safety & Security means that students generally feel safe, campus police are visible, blue light phones and escort services are readily available, and safety precautions are not overly necessary.

Computers

The Lowdown On...
Computers

High-Speed Network?
Yes.

Wireless Network?
Yes.

Number of Labs:
11

Number of Computers:
356

Operating Systems:
PC, MAC, and UNIX

Free Software:
Acrobat Reader
CodeWarrior Corporate Time
Maple
Mathematica
Matlab
Minitab
Mulberry
NiftyTelnet
Symantec Antivirus
Visual Studio server
Ethernet Campus Network

Discounted Software
Microsoft Office: $10

Windows XP: $10

24-Hour Labs
Baker 140

Cyert 100

Mellon 320a

Morewood

Wean 520

West Wing 109

Charge to Print?
No

Did You Know?

Carnegie Mellon was ranked the nation's most wired university in 2000 and 2001 in a Yahoo! Internet Life study.

New Computers!

Apple recently gifted the college 94 brand-new iMacs.

Students Speak Out On...
Computers

"Having your own computer is a must. CMU has tons of clusters with all different types of computers—Windows, Mac, UNIX, Sun—but having one in your room is really convenient. The wireless network at CMU is extensive. Basically, if you have a laptop, bring it, and you can access the internet from anywhere on campus."

Q "It's really convenient to bring your own computer. Sad but true, **most freshman network with other freshmen friends via Instant Messenger**. Also people check their e-mail every five minutes, so if you want to be a true CMU student, you'd need a computer for that. Also I'd recommend bringing a laptop because the school has wireless internet, so you can sit in class, outside, or in the library and be online. You'll be happier with a laptop, and you won't feel like an outsider!"

Q "**If you can afford a computer, bring one.** If you can't or don't want to, you'll still be fine. Occasionally, your life will be a living hell when everyone has a project due and all the campus printers are acting strange, but you can make it just fine without a computer. The clusters (labs) can get crowded, but if you budget your time well, which you most likely won't do, you don't need to sink more cash into a computer."

Q "I think **there are more computers at CMU than people per square foot.** There are a whole lot of public clusters and then your department will have their own private clusters. You can usually find a computer if you want one."

Q "Computer **labs are usually crowded**, but there are a lot so you'll be fine. It's nice, but every Sunday night, the network goes down for about seven hours."

Q "We are supposedly the most wired campus in the country. We have **seventeen computer clusters** and now even a wireless network—that means you can use the internet anywhere on campus; all you need is a wireless Ethernet card. This school is one of the best places to study computers, so we have good facilities for both Macs and PCs. You can usually find an open computer; if you can't in one place, a nearby cluster will have an open one. I have even heard rumors that if an enemy country wanted to drop a nuclear bomb on the U.S., CMU is one of the first targets because the CIA has headquarters and top-secret computers located here! I'm not sure if that's true."

Q "I'd say **we're pretty well-connected**. I'm not sure that it's good enough to be number one, but I think they do a good job. Most people get Ethernet connections, which are really fast. The computer clusters usually have quite a few people in it, but you'll almost always find your own computer to use. The computers at the clusters are fast because Intel is always donating stuff. The quality is good. I would advise you to bring your own computer, but then again, I'm a computer science major. If you're really into computers, you might prefer to bring a desktop. Pretty much all of the school has a wireless connection, which means you can go on the net from anywhere if you have a laptop. If you don't mind walking a little to get to a cluster when you want to use a computer, then there's no need to bring one."

Q "CMU is like **a planet of computers**. There are literally computers everywhere. There are so many computer clusters all over campus—in academic buildings, in dorms; they're everywhere! They're never really crowded, but I would suggest bringing your own computer for convenience. Our school is very computer-oriented. Professors post notes and homework online; quizzes and problem sets are online. It's just good to have, I guess."

Q "This is considered **the most wired campus in the country** because we were the first school to install a wireless network. I think there are actually more computers than students on this campus, so crowded labs are never a problem. I have my own computer, but I'm actually in a lab right now because this computer is much nicer and more up-to-date than mine. It's not necessary to have your own, although it can be a convenient."

Q "**Wireless is a Godsend.** There are computers everywhere. Clusters are not all that crowded until you get to the end of the semesters. People prefer to have their own computers. I would suggest getting a laptop since the wireless Ethernet on campus is definitely an advantage. We're all really computer savvy, so resources are not hard to come by normally. You can even rent laptop computers from the business school and the University Center for hours at a time."

The College Prowler Take On...
Computers

Yes, the wireless Ethernet network is great but it shouldn't overshadow the sheer volume of computers and computer supplies that are cascaded around campus. With so many computers, it's no surprise that students rarely have a problem finding an open computer in the cluster. It's true that many classes utilize the Blackboard website to post homework assignments, announcements, and grades. For some courses, students may have to check this site almost every day. The need to perpetually check your e-mail is another endearingly nerdy characteristic about CMU, and some students will start to get antsy if they can't access their accounts. There's a good reason for this however since professors will often e-mail students with news about class.

The campus is so computer-focused that it can be a little overbearing for the mouse-wielding novice. Eventually though, every student gets up to speed. If bringing a computer isn't a money issue, then make sure you bring one and make sure it's new. Technology becomes outdated even faster at CMU then it does in the real world. For students excited by the wireless network, a good laptop can be indispensable. When selecting a wireless card however, make sure to buy the University-recommended Orinoco card. It'll make getting on the campus network a lot easier for you. Computers are more than just machines at CMU; they're a way of life. You haven't experienced computer culture until you've come here.

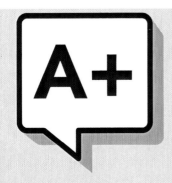

The College Prowler™ Grade on
Computers: A+

A high grade in Computers designates that computer labs are available, the computer network is easily accessible, and the campus' computing technology is up to date.

Facilities

The Lowdown On...
Facilities

Student Center:
The University Center (The UC)

Athletic Center:
The UC Gym
Skibo Gymnasium

Libraries:
Hunt Library
5 others

Popular Place to Chill:
Skibo Coffee House
The UC
The Fence

→

What Is There to Do On Campus?

In between classes you can break a sweat in the gym, cool off in the pool, take in a play, grab a bite to eat, or settle down to a $1 movie without ever leaving campus.

Movie Theatre on Campus?

Yes. McConomy Auditorium, The University Center

Bowling on Campus?

No.

Bar on Campus?

No. Although Panther Hollow Inn (PHI) is right down the street.

Coffeehouse on Campus?

Skibo Coffeehouse

The University Center

Favorite Things to Do On Campus?

The school shows a lot of movies, and these are very popular with students looking to relax for a few hours. Plays in the Purnell Center often draw larger crowds than most football games, and there's always someone in the computer clusters— whether they're doing work or playing a game. Skibo Coffeehouse often holds student readings and open mic. nights, and Rangos Hall (in the University Center) is host to concerts, guest speakers, dance competitions, and fashion shows.

> "The athletic facilities are mediocre. The free weight gym needs to be remodeled, but the track and football field have all-weather turf, which is nice. The student center is big, and it has a movie theater, a bookstore, a ton of clubs, a radio station, two pools, a gym, five squash courts, an aerobics room, a large stage for events, and many places to eat (but those get old pretty fast)."

"CMU has **the cleanest bathrooms** of any school I've ever seen. They're not cushy, but they're nice."

"Mostly **everything on campus seems to be newly-re-modeled.** Since we have such a big computer department at our school, computer companies fight to give us computers. We have brand-new Macs and IBMs in all the labs. The gym is pretty nice, but if you are a hardcore athlete and you workout a lot, you may have to wait for a machine once in a while."

"The computer places are good. I've never used the athletic stuff, although they seem decent for a fairly un-athletic school. Part of CMU's problem is that **it doesn't have one main gathering area for students to meet and build a student community.** Therefore, school unity suffers and the school becomes segregated into clicks which mingle on occasion."

Q "They show **movies in the University Center** on a big screen for a dollar; that's always nice."

Q "The athletic facilities are very nice. We have a 25-meter pool, track, football field, and other things. Overall, the campus layout is nice because **everything is very close**, but housing services is very lacking in the speed of fixing things."

Q "There are **a couple of gyms that are okay.** We have all the fields and facilities you could really want, and they do the job even if they aren't billion-dollar facilities."

Q "The gym is nice, although it gets pretty crowded during peak hours. **I think CMU should definitely spend more money** on their facilities."

Q "**The weight room is small**, and there are some exercise classes you can take. I find that it all suits my needs. I just take a few aerobics classes a week. In the University Center, you have a small bookstore and a convenience store that are both open fairly late. There's limited stuff, but it's sufficient."

Q "The UC is a place to come hang out, but as of right now, **there's not too much to do** there besides relax and eat."

Q "**We have a very nice swimming pool**, indoor racquetball/ squash courts, tennis courts, and a football field. We also have a nice student center that was recently built."

Q "I think the facilities are pretty nice. **There is always con- struction being done on campus** because they're always trying to improve what we have. The student center is only about five years old. The architecture is a little weird, but it's huge, new, and inviting. Computers are always state-of-the-art, and I swear that there are more of them than there are students."

Q "**The athletics facilities are good.** They have some pretty good gyms, and they're usually not too crowded, especially compared to other schools I've been to. The computer clusters are good; they pay a lot of money to let everyone use some expensive software. The student center is probably good if you want to get involved with that, but I couldn't say much, because I'm not."

The College Prowler Take On...
Facilities

The University Center is the focal point of campus life at CMU. It contains numerous eateries, a gym, basketball court, and meeting rooms. It's also a great place to just sit and chill between classes. The UC is only a few years old, and the building itself is an impressive piece of architecture. Athletic facilities in the UC include an enormous basketball court/gymnasium, a small but well-equipped weight room, five racquetball courts, and an aerobics room. Skibo Gym, a larger athletic facility, is also located on campus. Skibo is an old, poorly-maintained gym that attracts dedicated weightlifters.

On the whole, the campus is aesthetically pleasing. Some students have even said that the College of Fine Arts building is the reason why they came to Carnegie Mellon. It is a stunning structure to be enjoyed by all students, but it's casual yet austere air is most compatible with art, design, and architecture majors. There are also some buildings that reflect the campus' industrial bent. The dank and stale Wean Hall is the largest poured concrete building in the country. It's also one of the most repulsive, but you won't see that on any fact sheets. It's recommended to tour the campus before attending CMU. Most prospective students are charmed by its quaint yet busy atmosphere, but some find the buildings to be a bit ugly.

The College Prowler™ Grade on

Facilities: B-

A high Facilities grade indicates that the campus is aesthetically pleasing and well maintained, facilities are state-of-the-art, and libraries are exceptional. Other determining factors include the quality of both athletic and student centers and an abundance of things to do on campus.

Campus Dining

The Lowdown On...
Campus Dining

Freshman Meal Plan Requirement?

Yes

Meal Plan Average Cost:

$3,650

Places to Grab a Bite with Your Meal Plan:

The Original Hot Dog Shop
Location: UC
Food: American
Favorite Dish: Cheese Dog with Fries
Mon-Sun 11 a.m.-2 a.m.

Pepperazi
Location: UC
Food: Italian
Favorite Dish: Baked Pasta w/ Cheese
Mon-Sun 11 a.m.-10 p.m.

Barista Café
Location: UC
Food: Coffee/Bakery
Favorite Dish: Bagel with Flavored Cream Cheese
Mon-Fri 8 a.m.-7 p.m.
Sat-Sun 8 a.m.-10:30 a.m. and 4 p.m.-7 p.m.

➔

CK's Pretzels
Location: UC
Food: Pretzels, Sushi, and Shakes
Favorite Dish: California Roll
Mon-Fri 10:30 a.m.-7p.m.

La Prima
Location: Baker Hall, Purnell Center, Wean Hall
Food: Coffee/Pastries
Favorite Drink: Espresso
Mon-Fri 8 a.m.-4 p.m.

Si Senor
Location: UC
Food: Southwest/Mexican
Favorite Dish: Chicken Cilantro Quesadilla
Mon-Fri 11 a.m.-9 p.m.
Sat-Sun 11 a.m.-4 p.m.

East Street Deli
Location: UC
Food: Sandwiches/Breakfast
Favorite Dish: Smoked Turkey Sandwich with Pesto Mayo Sauce
Mon-Sun 8 a.m.-7 p.m.

Main Street Market
Location: Newell-Simon
Food: American
Favorite Dish: Pepperoni Pizza
Mon-Fri 8 a.m.-3 p.m.

The Underground
Location: Morewood E-Tower
Food: Sandwiches/Soups
Favorite Dish: Cheeseburger
Mon-Sun 11 a.m.-11 p.m.

Taste of India
Location: Resnik and Old Student Center
Food: Indian
Favorite Dish: Chicken Curry
Sun-Fri 11 a.m.-2 p.m. and 4:30 p.m.-9 p.m.

Asiana
Location: Newell-Simon
Food: Chinese
Favorite Dish: BarbeGrill Chicken
Mon-Thur: 11 a.m.-7 p.m.
Fri 11 a.m.-4 p.m.

Ginger's Deli
Location: Posner Hall
Food: Sandwiches/Soups
Favorite Dish: Soup of the Day
Mon-Fri 8 a.m.-3 p.m.

Penne's Int'l Market Place
Location: UC
Food: Various
Favorite Dish: Value Meal
Mon-Sun 11 a.m.-7 p.m.

Schatz Dining Hall
Location: UC
Food: Buffet Style
Breakfast Hours:
Mon-Fri 7:30 a.m.-10:30 a.m.
Sun Brunch: 10 a.m.-2 p.m.

Dinner Hours:
Select Tuesdays, Wednesdays, and Thursdays 5 p.m.-7 p.m.

Off-Campus Places to Use Your Meal Plan:

Subway
415 S. Craig St., Oakland
(412) 687-6728

Pizza Outlet
3608 Fifth Ave., Oakland
(412) 687-4666

The Original Hot Dog Shop
3901 Forbes Ave., Oakland
(412) 621-7388

Eat'n Park
1816 Murray Ave., Squirrel Hill
(412) 422-7203

Student Favorites
Si Senor, Taste of India, The Original Hot Dog Shop

Did You Know?

Ever go traying? When it snows, CMU kids will steal the cafeteria trays and use them to go sledding on the hills behind Donner Hall and in Schenley Park.

Students Speak Out On...
Campus Dining

"The thing I dislike the most about CMU is that there is no central dining hall. As a freshman, I thought the food was OK. As a sophomore, I got sick of it pretty quickly and started eating off campus as much as possible."

Q "The food is **overpriced and causes malnutrition**. It's impossible to eat enough on campus if you're vegetarian or kosher."

Q "Food is OK. **If you are a vegetarian, you may have some qualms,** but check out Si Senor. I ate there every night my freshman year. Also Skibo has a lot of healthy food and veggie food. Skibo also plays music, and it achieves a college coffee house atmosphere. I recommend checking it out. Usually, people decide to come to CMU just because of Skibo. It's those same students who end up working there and creating their own smoothies. There's also an all-you-can-eat buffet some nights each week if you want to gorge. The Underground is only an OK place to eat, but it's a very cool place to hang out. It's under Morewood—a freshman dorm—so that's a convenient place."

Q "**The food sucks.** The school has made a huge effort to diversify the selection of food, and in the process has made it so confusing and crappy that being on the meal plan is a hassle. You look forward to the times of day when you don't have to eat at the irritating establishments around campus. The meal plan is of poor value, overly complicated, and worst of all, it's very unsatisfying because the food is always too greasy, too bland, too overcooked, or too weird. The Chinese restaurant in Newell-Simon is one of the better spots, and sometimes the pizza in the University Center is good. The best dining on campus is the selection of vans parked next to Posner Hall—there's Chinese, Thai, Greek, and Indian. It's all fresh and fairly tasty and at a very good value."

Q "Since I'm in my fifth year, I don't know how the food is anymore, but I hear **it has gotten a lot better**. Posner Hall has a place to eat which is good; it has sandwiches and soups and two different hot meals each day. The University Center food is all right; it really depends on what you like. There is a large variety there like Mexican, American, Middle Eastern, Italian, chicken, and bagels."

Q "The food is okay on campus, although **it's a little expensive** through the required first-year meal plan. It is varied. We have Indian, Chinese, Italian, and Mexican, as well as sandwiches, pizza, and normal American food. I'm happy with the meal situation here, although I'm not very picky."

Q "The food on campus (for the most part) sucks. **I eat mostly off campus or what I cook myself.** There is stuff in the University Center that is good for snacking and some are at reasonable prices, but a lot of it is overpriced. Personally, if I have to eat on campus, I will eat at one of two places. This guy named Sree sells Indian food out of a van over by Posner Hall; I know that sounds bad, but a lot of people do it. There are at least four or five places around campus, so anyways, this is good food, you get a lot of it, and it's cheap—four bucks gets you a fairly large meal plus a drink. You can't beat that!"

Q "**The food on campus really sucks**, and I'm sure most people will tell you that. If you come, get as few meal plans as possible with money to spend wherever. Anyways, most people skip some meals and have a lot of their weekly plan leftover by Sunday. It doesn't carry over, so I bought a giant pack of orange juice the last day because I had so much leftover that I needed to spend it."

Q "**I don't know anyone who likes the food on campus.**
And they make you eat on campus for the first year. This
can be either bad or good. It's bad because you're forced
to pay high prices and eat their food. It's good because
you won't be starved and there's a very good chance that
you'll eat more than you would otherwise. Regardless,
after the first year, you can get off the school plan (which
is what everyone does) and then use your money however
you want. It's always nice to go to some place close to
school where you can eat well."

Q "Food is surprisingly really good at CMU. I've visited a lot
of my friends at other colleges and their food just sucks.
We have a wide variety, ranging from Mexican food, to a
deli, to fried food, and also Indian and Chinese food. We
pretty much have everything, and it's not bad either."

Q "I think every school has their ups and downs with food.
The food at CMU is relatively good. It all tastes good.
I'm not sure how healthy some of the food is, but I think
everyone finds something that they like. After a while, I
found that I get really tired of having the same food over
and over, but they're supposedly changing the dining.
Usually, students end their meal plan after the first year.
I'm staying on it. The meal plan goes like this: You have
a certain number of blocks, and then you have a certain
amount of Dinex (basically, it's money you can use at any-
time on campus until you run out)."

Q "There are little trucks that sit in the street on campus,
and those are the places to hit up for lunch—it's mostly
Chinese, Thai, etc. It's pretty good food! Other than that,
there are places to eat on campus, but there are so many
places to walk to, **I'd rather go off campus.**"

Q "The campus dining experience **leaves a lot to be
desired**. Food plans have changed a lot since I've been
there, but you need to go for the plan that gives you the
most flexibility—Dine Express, or Dinex, is much better

than meal blocks. The many food carts around the streets are very popular. Sree's Indian food is probably the best of these. There's also The Original Hot Dog Shop (which is ironically not an original but a copy of the identical shop which is just down Forbes Avenue on Pitt's campus). They have the greasiest, yet best, French fries ever."

All but the most optimistic student has problems with campus dining. Fixing the dining situation is a big problem for the University and an even bigger hassle for the students. There is currently no all-you-can-eat dining hall, and on-campus dining consists of individual campus-run restaurants. Here, the meal plan provides you with two ways to pay. A "block" is a unit of credit that's good for one whole meal. The other way to pay, Dine Extra, works like cash but can only be used to buy campus food. The average meal will cost you about $7. Freshmen are required to be on the meal plan and most are unhappy with it. Fortunately, students can structure their meal plan to provide themselves with the most flexibility by choosing how much money to allot to block units and how much money to allot to Dine Extra.

The most disappointing thing about eating on campus is the small amount of food you receive for the high price you pay. The food isn't all bad. Although a dining hall would be nice, the lack of one means that CMU students don't have to suffer through cafeteria-style food. Asiana and Si Senor offer some delicious dishes, and The Original Hot Dog Shop offers some of the tastiest artery-clogging food in town. For freshmen year, the meal plan is bearable, but after that, most students stay off campus when grabbing a bite to eat.

The College Prowler™ Grade on

Campus Dining: C-

Our grade on Campus Dining addresses the quality of both school-owned dining halls and independent on campus restaurants as well as the price, availability, and variety of food available.

Off-Campus Dining

The Lowdown On...
Off-Campus Dining

Restaurant Prowler:

Popular Places to Eat!

Buffalo Blues
216 S. Highland Ave., Shadyside
(412) 362-5837
Food: American/BBQ
Price: $10 and under per person
Mon-Sat 11 a.m.-2 a.m.
Sun 12 p.m.-2 a.m

Casbah
229 S. Highland Ave., Shadyside
(412) 661-5656

Food: Italian/Mediterranean
Price: $25 and under per person
Mon-Thur 11:30 a.m.-2:30 p.m.
and 5 p.m.-10 p.m.
Fri 11:30 a.m.-2:30 p.m. and 5
p.m.-11 p.m.
Sat 5 p.m.-11 p.m.
Sun 11 a.m.-2:30 p.m. and 5 p.m.-
9 p.m.

China Palace
5440 Walnut St., Shadyside
(412) 687-RICE
Food: Chinese
Price: $15 and under per person
Mon-Fri 11:30 a.m.-10 p.m.

Sat 11:30 a.m.-11 p.m.
Sun 2 p.m.-9 p.m.

Cozumel
5505 Walnut St., Shadyside
(412) 621-5100
Food: Mexican
Cool Features: Dancing
Price: $15 and under per person
Mon-Fri 11 a.m.-2:30 p.m. and 5 p.m.-10 p.m.
Sat 12 p.m.-10 p.m.
Sun 12 p.m.-9 p.m.

Fuel & Fuddle
212 Oakland Ave., Oakland
(412) 682-3473
Food: American
Cool Features: Live music and poetry readings
Price: $10 and under per person
Mon-Sun 11 a.m.-2 a.m.

India Garden
328 Atwood St., Oakland
(412) 682-3000
Food: Indian
Price: $15 and under per person
Mon-Sun 11 a.m.-1 a.m.

Joe Mama's
3716 Forbes Ave., Oakland
(412) 621-7282
Food: Italian
Price: $15 and under per person
Mon-Sat 11 a.m.-11 p.m.

Sun 11 a.m.-4 p.m.
Bar: Mon-Sun until 2 a.m.

Lucca
317 S. Craig St.
(412) 682-3310
Food: Italian
Cool Features: Outdoor Dining
Price: $25 and under per person
Mon-Wed 11 a.m.-2:30 p.m. and 5 p.m.-10 p.m.
Fri-Sat 11 a.m.-2:30 p.m. and 5 p.m.-11 p.m.

LuLu's Noodles
400 S. Craig St., Oakland
(412) 681-3333
Food: Asian
Price: $15 and under per person
Mon-Sun 11 a.m.-10 p.m.

Mad Mex
370 Atwood St., Oakland
(412) 681-5656
Food: Mexican
Price: $10 and under per person
Mon-Sun 11 a.m.-2 a.m.

Max and Erma's
5533 Walnut St., Shadyside
(412) 681-5775
Food: American
Price: $15 and under per person
Mon-Fri 11:30 a.m.-10 p.m.
Sat-Sun 11:30 a.m.-11 p.m.

Shady Grove/Walnut Grill
5500 Walnut St., Shadyside
(412) 69-0909
Food: American/Eclectic
Price: $15 and under per person
11 a.m.-2 a.m.

Thai Place Café
301 S. Craig St., Oakland
(412) 622-0133
Food: Thai
Price: $15 and under per person
Mon-Sat 10:30 a.m.-9:30 p.m.
Closed Sundays.

Union Grill
413 S. Craig St., Oakland
(412) 681-8620
Food: American
Cool Features: Outdoor Dining,
good happy hour specials
Price: $15 and under per person
Mon-Sat 11:30 a.m.-12 p.m.
Sun 11:30 a.m.-9 p.m.

Village Pizza
810 Ivy St., Shadyside
(412) 682-6878
Food: American/Italian
Price: $10 and under per person
Mon-Tue 11 a.m.-2 a.m.
Wed-Sat 11 a.m.-2 a.m.
Sun 12 p.m.-2 a.m.

Sushi Too
5432 Walnut St., Shadyside
(412) 687-8744
Food: Japanese

Price: $15 and under per person-
Mon-Sat 11:30 a.m.-2 p.m. and 5
p.m.-10 p.m.
Sun 4 p.m.-9 p.m.

Monterey Bay Fish Grotto
1411 Grandview Ave.
(412) 481-4414
Food: Seafood
Price: $25 and under per person
Mon-Thur 11 a.m.-10 p.m.
Fri 11 a.m.-12 a.m.
Sat 4 p.m.-10 p.m.

New Dumpling House
2138 Murray Ave., Squirrel Hill
(412) 422-4178
Food: Chinese/Japanese
Price: $15 and under per person
Mon-Thur 11 a.m.-10 p.m.
Fri-Sat 11 a.m.-10 p.m.
Sun 11 a.m.-10 p.m.

Orient Kitchen
4808 Baum Blvd., Shadyside
(412) 682-3311
Food: Asian
Price: $15 and under per person
Sun-Thur 11 a.m.-1 a.m.
Fri-Sat 11 a.m.-2 a.m

Pamela's
3703 Forbes Ave., Oakland
(412) 683-4066
Food: American/Breakfast
5527 Walnut St., Shadyside
8 a.m.-4 p.m., Sun 9 a.m.-3 p.m.

Pittsburgh Deli Company
728 Copeland St., Shadyside
(412) 682-3354
Food: Sandwiches
Price: $10 and under per person
Daily 11 a.m.-2 a.m.

Primanti Brothers
3803 Forbes Ave., Oakland
(412) 621-4444
Food: American/Fast Food
Price: $10 and under per person
Mon-Wed 10 a.m.-2 a.m.
Thur-Sat 11 a.m.-3 a.m.
Sun 11 a.m.-12 a.m.

Late-Night, Half-Price Food Specials:
Fuel & Fuddle
India Garden
Joe Mama's
Mad Mex
PDC

24-Hour Eating?
Eat'n Park
Ritter's Diner
Tom's Diner

Did You Know?

Fun Facts:
Big Macs, Heinz Ketchup, and Klondike Bars were all invented in Pittsburgh.

Ever have a pierogie?
Usually stuffed with potatoes, cheese, or sauerkraut, these dumplings are a Pittsburgh staple thanks to the city's Polish heritage.

Want a Pittsburgh-style salad?
Just add fries.

Best Place to Take Your Parents:

Lucca

Casbah

Monterey Bay Fish Grotto

Best Pizza:

Village Pizza

Best Chinese:

Orient Kitchen

LuLu's Noodles

China Palace

Best Breakfast:

Pamela's

Best Wings:

Buffalo Blues

Quaker Steak and Lube

PHI

Redbeards

Best Healthy:

Craig Street Coffee

Jen's Juice Joint

Whole Food

Closest Grocery Stores:

Giant Eagle

4612 Centre Ave., Oakland

(412) 681-1500

Giant Eagle

4250 Murray Ave., Squirrel Hill

(412) 421-8161

Students Speak Out On...
Off-Campus Dining

"There are a lot of restaurants within close proximity of campus, and there are even more if you are willing to take the bus, which is free for CMU students. My favorite place to eat is at the Waterfront. It's about ten minutes away by bus and has lots of restaurants. Subway, my personal favorite for a quick meal, is very close to campus as well."

Q "**There are a bunch of good eats.** In Oakland, check out Fuel & Fuddle at night; it's half-price after 11 p.m., and it's a real college place. In Squirrel Hill, go to Aladdin's—it has all kinds of Middle Eastern food, and everything on the menu is super tasty. LuLu's is my friend's favorite place; sometimes he eats there several times a day. It's pretty close to campus and has Pan-Asian food, whatever that means. Craig Street Coffee is pretty good too!"

Q "Restaurants off campus are decent. Sometimes **it can be frustrating to eat pizza and subs all the time,** but truthfully the CMU area of Pittsburgh has some pretty affordable places to eat where things don't taste too bad."

Q "**Restaurants with waiters and waitresses don't exist on campus,** but off campus on the University of Pittsburgh's campus in Oakland (a ten-minute walk from CMU), there are a bunch of good restaurants. Fuel & Fuddle and Mad Mex are half-price after 11 p.m., which is a big thing for students."

Q "We're right in a city, so **eating off campus is great**. There are three neighborhoods around us with great places: Oakland, Squirrel Hill, and Shadyside. Craig Street is right by campus and has lots of great places. I don't like to recommend one restaurant because I'm all about experimenting."

Q "I found that a lot of the restaurants off campus are really good; **they have a lot of Indian and Chinese**. The pizza's awful! But I guess I'm just spoiled coming from New York and all. Oh my God, go to LuLu's! It's the best Chinese food I have ever had! And Pino's and Gulifty's are all really good places. Joe Mama's and Fuel & Fuddle have half-off food nights as well."

Q "There are lots of great places in Pittsburgh; the city is as diverse as the school. In fact, I go to new places all the time. **There's a great Italian place called Claudio's**. Pittsburgh really has everything. You can even get Kosher Chinese food."

Q "The restaurants aren't bad. There's fast food all over the place. In addition, there are Italian places call Pi and Pino's in Squirrel Hill, a nice Italian place in Shadyside called Pasta Piatta, an American place in Shadyside called Max and Erma's, **some fun places in Oakland where you can get half-priced food**, and lots of yummy places downtown. There is really a wide spectrum of stuff."

Q "**Hemingway's has half-price food between 9 p.m. and 12 a.m**. and LuLu's is not that expensive. You can eat the old fast-food stuff, but I guess there's nothing new about that"

The College Prowler Take On...
Off-Campus Dining

Off-campus dining provides students with a diverse palette of foods to choose from. Just about every student has their own favorite restaurant. It's hard for students to decide exactly where to eat sometimes with so many delectable dining options. Students love places that offer half-price dining (Fuel & Fuddle, Joe Mama's, India Garden, Pittsburgh Deli Company, Hemingway's, and Mad Mex). Not only do these establishments offer students great prices, but their culinary creations are plentiful and delicious. Most every student agrees that Lu-Lu's is the best Chinese food in the area. The amount of food you get for the price you pay is very generous. Sushi Too in Shadyside is a great place for all kinds of Japanese food, not just sushi, and right down the street at Cozumel you can find a lively environment and some spicy Mexican cuisine. Leaving the campus to dine out is a joy for most students!

Compared with the extremely poor condition of on-campus dining, eating off-campus becomes even more appealing. If there's one downside, it's that students are usually too busy to leave campus for an enjoyable sit-down meal. As a student, you may find yourself eating at one place over and over again simply because it's convenient. Too bad it seems to be the case that Pittsburgh doesn't have a definitive "best place for pizza." Students should explore the local dining scene though, as it can yield some sumptuous results.

A-

The College Prowler™ Grade on

Off-Campus
Dining: A-

"A high off campus dining grade implies that off campus restaurants are affordable, accessible, and worth visiting. Other factors include the variety of cuisine and the availability of alternative options (vegetarian, vegan, kosher, etc.)"

On-Campus Housing

The Lowdown On...
On-Campus Housing

Room Types:

Residence Rooms include standard, prime, and suite-style units.

Standard--students share a large, central bathroom facility (most first-year students are assigned to these rooms);

Prime--students share a private or semi-private bathroom with no more than five students;

Suite-style--students share a semi-private bathroom and a common living area.

Apartments are located both on and off campus. These units can be efficiencies, one-bedrooms, or two-bedroom apartments and have in-room kitchens.

Houses are mainly on campus and include bedrooms, a kitchen, dining rooms, living rooms, private bathrooms, and laundry facilities. Many houses are reserved for special interests or associations.

Dormitories:

Boss House

Floors: 3 + Basement

Total Occupancy: 71

Bathrooms: In-Room

Coed: No

% of Men/Women: 100/0

% of First-Year Students: 48

Room Types: Prime Single, Prime Double

Special Features: Recreation Area, Television Room, Study Lounge, Laundry

Doherty Apartments

Floors: 3 + Basement

Total Occupancy: 151

Bathrooms: In-Room

Coed: Yes

% of Men/Women: 42/58

% of First-Year Students: 17

Room Types: Efficiency, 1 Bedroom, 2 Bedroom

Special Features: Recreation Area, Television Room, Laundry

Donner House

Floors: 3 + A Level

Total Occupancy: 252

Bathrooms: Shared by Floor

Coed: Yes

% of Men/Women: 63/37

% of First-Year Students: 88

Room Types: Standard Single, Standard Double, Standard Triple

Special Features: Recreation Area, Television Room, Study Lounge, Laundry, Ping-Pong, Pool Table

Hamerschlag House

Floors: 3

Total Occupancy: 168

Bathrooms: Shared by Floor

Coed: No

% of Men/Women: 100/0

% of First-Year Students: 96

Room Types: Standard Single, Prime Single, Standard Double

Special Features: Television/ Recreation Area, Common Kitchen, Laundry, Pool Table

Henderson House

(Recently Renovated)

Floors: 3 + Ground Level

Total Occupancy: 60

Bathrooms: In-Room

Coed: Yes

% of Men/Women: 34/66

% of First-Year Students: 63

Room Types: Prime Single, Prime Double

Special Features: Recreation Area, Television Room, Study Lounge, Laundry, Wellness Housing

Margaret Morrison Apartments

Floors: 3

Total Occupancy: 30

Bathroom: Shared by Apartment House

Coed: Yes

% of Men/Women: n/a

% of First-Year Students: n/a

Room Types: Prime Double

Special Features: Margaret Morrison is Only Available to Students Receiving Special Interest Housing, Access to Computer Cluster, Laundry

McGill House

Floors: 3 + Basement

Total Occupancy: 72

Bathroom: In-Room

Coed: No

% of Men/Women: 0/100

% of First-Year Students: 36

Room Types: Prime Single, Prime Double

Special Features: Recreation Area, Television Room, Study Lounge, Laundry

Morewood Gardens A-D Tower

Floors: 7

Total Occupancy: 677

Bathrooms: In-Room

Coed: Yes

% of Men/Women: 50/50

% of First-Year Students: 55

Room Types: Efficiency, Prime Single, Prime Double, Prime Triple, Prime Quad, Standard Single, Standard Double

Special Features: Recreation Room, Television Room, Study Lounge, Laundry, Computer Cluster, Mail Room Common Kitchen

Morewood Gardens E-Tower

Floors: 4

Total Occupancy: 210

Bathrooms: Shared by Floor

Coed: Yes

% of Men/Women: 50/50

% of First-Year Students: 100

Room Types: Standard Single, Standard Double

Special Features: Study Lounge, Laundry

Mudge House

Floors: 3 + Basement

Total Occupancy: 311

Bathrooms: In-Room

Coed: Yes

% of Men/Women: 65/35

% of First-Year Students: 27

Room Types: House, Efficiency, Prime Single, Prime Double, Prime Triple, Prime Quad, Standard Single, Standard Double, Standard Triple

Features: Living Room, Dining Room, Parlor Room, Study Lounge, Television Room, Garden Courtyard, Laundry, Mailroom, Common Kitchen

New House

Floors: 5

Total Occupancy: 256

Bathrooms: Shared by Floor

Coed: Yes

% of Men/Women: n/a

% of First-Year Students: 100

Room Types: n/a

Features: Conference Room, Laundry, Fitness Room

Resnik House

Floors: 5

Total Occupancy: 151

Bathrooms: In-Room

Coed: Yes

% of Men/Women: 64/36

% of First-Year Students: 7

Room Types: Prime Single, Prime Double, Suite Single, Suite Double

Features: Air Conditioned, Television Room, Computer Cluster, Mailroom

Roselawn Terrace Houses

Floors: 2 Floors + Basement per House

Total Occupancy: 60

Bathrooms: In-House

Coed: Yes

% of Men/Women: 58/42

% of First-Year Students: 2

Room Types: House

Features: Kitchen, Living Room, Dining Room, Laundry

Scobell House

Floors: 3 + A-Level

Total Occupancy: 86

Bathrooms: Shared by Floor

Coed: No

% of Men/Women: 100/0

% of First-Year Students: 80

Room Types: Standard Single, Standard Double, Prime Single, Prime Single

Features: Lounge, Laundry

West Wing

Floors: 5

Total Occupancy: 147

Bathrooms: In-Room

Coed: Yes

% of Men/Women: 67/33

% of First-Year Students: 5

Room Types: Prime Single, Prime Double, Suite Single, Suite Double

Features: Air Conditioned, Television Room, Computer Cluster, Mailroom

Woodlawn Apartments

Floors: 3 Floors + Basement

Total Occupancy: 34

Bathrooms: In-Room

Coed: Yes

% of Men/Women: 53/47

% of First-Year Students: 21

Room Types: 1 Bedroom, 2 Bedroom, 4 Bedroom

Features: Laundry, Art Gallery

Cathedral Mansions

Total Occupancy: 296

Bathrooms: In-Room

Coed: Yes

% of Men/Women: 54/46

% of First-Year Students: 31

Room Types: Efficiency, 1 Bedroom, 2 Bedroom

Features: Kitchen, Laundry

Fairfax Apartments

Total Occupancy: 112

Bathrooms: In-Room

Coed: Yes

% of Men/Women: 59/41

% of First-Year Students: 23

Room Types: Efficiency, 1 Bedroom, 2 Bedroom

Features: Kitchen, Laundry, Workout Room

London Terrace Apartments

Total Occupancy: 40

Bathrooms: In-Room

Coed: Yes

% of Men/Women: n/a

% of First-Year Students: n/a

Room Types: Efficiency, 1 Bedroom

Features: Kitchen, Laundry

James Manor

Total Occupancy: 24

Bathrooms: In-Room

Coed: Yes

% of Men/Women: n/a

% of First-Year Students: n/a

Room Types: 2 Bedroom

Features: Kitchen, Laundry

Saxony Apartments

Total Occupancy: 44

Bathrooms: In-Room

Coed: Yes

% of Men/Women: n/a

% of First-Year Students: n/a

Room Types: Efficiency, 1 Bedroom, 2 Bedroom

Features: Kitchen, Laundry, Garage Parking (additional charge)

Marybelle Apartments

Total Occupancy: 36

Bathrooms: In-Room

Coed: Yes

% of Men/Women: 86/14

% of First-Year Students: 0

Room Types: Efficiency

Features: Kitchen, Laundry

Welch House

Floors: 3

Total Occupancy: 56

Bathrooms: In-Room

Coed: Yes

% of Men/Women: 55/45

% of First-Year Students: 25

Room Types: Prime Single, Prime Double

Features: Television and Study Lounge, Parlor Room, Laundry, Quiet Living Area

Shady Oak Apartments

Total Occupancy: 71

Bathrooms: In-Room

Coed: Yes

% of Men/Women: 48/52

% of First-Year Students: 4

Room Types: Efficiency, 1 Bedroom, 2 Bedroom

Features: Kitchen, Laundry

Shirley Apartments

Total Occupancy: 41

Bathrooms: In-Room

Coed: Yes

% of Men/Women: 70/30

% of First-Year Students: 20

Room Types: Efficiency, 1 Bedroom, Prime Single

Features: Kitchen, Laundry

Webster Hall

Total Occupancy: 118

Bathrooms: In-Room

Coed: Yes

% of Men/Women: 58/42

% of First-Year Students: 32

Room Types: 1 Bedroom, 2
Bedroom

Features: Kitchen, Laundry

with some singles.

Did You Know?
All campus residents get free cable and access to
CMU's movie channel.

Best Dorms:

Morewood Gardens

Mudge House

New House

Resnik

West Wing

Worst Dorms:

Scobell

Boss

Donner

Hamerschlag

Undergrads on Campus:
72%

Bed Type:
Twin extra long (39"x80"); some lofts, some bunk-beds

Available for Rent:
Mini Fridge with Microwave

Cleaning Service?
In public areas. Community and semi-private bathrooms are cleaned by staff approximately once a week. Community Apartment bathrooms are not cleaned.

You Get:
bed, desk and chair, bookshelf, dresser, closet or wardrobe, window coverings, cable TV jack, Ethernet or broadband inter- net connections, free campus and local phone calls

Also Available:
Smoke-free living option, special-interest housing

Students Speak Out On...
On-Campus Housing

"The dorms are pretty nice here. For fresh-men, Morewood E-Tower and New House are really nice, but they have communal bathrooms. Mudge is great because it's mostly first-years and you share a bath-room with one other person. Donner is . . . ugly."

Q "The dorms are OK, but **most are too small.** It's hard to get your own single with your own kitchen and bath-room."

Q "The dorms are really nice. There is a new dorm (New House) that is LEED certified—that is a rating system for environmental or green buildings. Morewood E-Tower is all freshmen. There are food and mail rooms in that dorm. Mudge is nice, and it's only a bit further away from cam-pus than Morewood. Donner is all freshmen too, but **stay away from the basement, they call it The Dungeon.**"

Q "The dorms are just OK. Supposedly they're much larger than other school's dorms. **They're still real crusty though.** Do not live in Donner! It is a stinking cesspool. Morewood is de-cent, along with Mudge and Doherty apartments. Get off cam-pus and into local apartments or houses as soon as possible."

Q "Donner is a great dorm for first-years to meet people and be social, but there are community showers and whatnot. Some don't like that and the fact that the building is green. **More-wood is cool, because a lot of people live there.** E-Tower is for freshmen. Resnik is awful for freshmen."

Q "Morewood and Mudge are nice because they are coed and near the fraternity quad. Donner looks good on the inside, but is pretty ugly on the outside; it's coed as well. **Stay away from the Hill dorms:** Boss, McGill, Hamerschlag, and Scobell."

Q "The dorms are fine. I lived in Donner Hall my freshman year and had an on-campus apartment sophomore year. **I loved living in Donner.** At first, I was wary of community bathrooms, but it was actually pretty cool because that's where I met my best friends. Sometimes the different majors can be isolated, especially in the College of Fine Arts, so it was great to get to know students from all departments. In fact, my current roommate is a lovely civil engineering major, someone I would have never met if I didn't live in a standard double my first year. That's what I recommend as a first-year student. Living in prime housing (where you share a bathroom with two or three other people) doesn't help you meet other kids. Then once you know people, you can move into an apartment of prime rooms. I recommend Donner Hall because it has the biggest rooms and the best sense of community of any of the dorms."

Q "I was in an off-campus apartment called Shirley for the first two weeks. **It was rough**—the walking and being in an environment with like thirty-eight out of forty-one people that were upperclassmen—but now I'm in Morewood, and it's great. Anything on campus is good. Don't request Donner because that's a crappy dorm."

Q "In general, **the dorms are decent.** There aren't many singles, so get used to the idea that you're going to have a roommate. The only freshman dorm that I'd stay away from is Donner because they have a public potty and its looks like a gym on the inside."

Q "Stay away from Donner. **Morewood sucks too**, but that's the best chance you have of getting laid at 3 a.m. when you're walking back home drunk from a party. Most freshmen live in Morewood because of that."

Q "**Resnik and West Wing are the best dorms**, I think. But they're usually taken over by juniors and seniors, so it's almost impossible to get in there, especially if you're a freshman. I think Mudge House is pretty neat, but it's like ten minutes across the street from the center of the campus, so it's a little off from what I want in my dorm, but you may like it very much. It looks nice. I suggest you avoid Donner Hall and Hamerschlag House. Hamerschlag is all-male. Although I would hate to live in Donner, I think people learn to live with it in time."

The College Prowler Take On...
On-Campus Housing

All freshmen are required to live on campus. Most students are thankful for their experience in the dorms and feel that they wouldn't have adjusted well to life at CMU without it. It's hard to find a freshman that lived in Morewood E-Tower (a first-year dorm) and didn't have a great time. E-tower can sometimes seem like the social nexus of the freshman universe. Students from other dorms will even come over just to hang out. Reactions to another freshman-filled dorm, Donner, are mixed. Residents of Donner often build an unflinching solidarity and love for "Big Blue." Students who've stayed elsewhere, however, just find the dormitory to be an eyesore. Community apartment housing is fully-furnished, equipped with a kitchen, and close to campus, but freshmen who've been placed there often express feelings of being out of the social loop.

The dorms are inviting and well-furnished, especially compared to most other colleges and universities. The bathrooms are sufficient, and the showers are spacious. The beds aren't uncomfortable either, but you may find yourself sleeping tenuous inches from the ceiling on a platform bed/desk combination. In that case, be prepared to bump your head most mornings. For the first part of freshman year, it's not uncommon to see students polarized into different social groups based on their residence hall. The University even stresses this division with a Dorm Wars competition during orientation week. For first-year students, pride in their dorm can be very important. As a freshman, you'll want to live in first-year housing, as it provides a social atmosphere and the most affable students. This means living in Morewood E-Tower, New House, Donner, or some of the all-freshman floors in Mudge.

The College Prowler™ Grade on
Campus Housing: D

A high Campus Housing grade indicates that dorms are clean, well-maintained and spacious. Other determining factors include variety of dorms, proximity to classes and social atmosphere.

Off-Campus Housing

The Lowdown On...
Off-Campus Housing

Undergrads in Off-Campus Housing:
28%

Average Rent for a Studio Apartment:
$500 per month

Average Rent for a One-Bedroom Apartment:
$600 per month

Average Rent for a Two-Bedroom Apartment:
$850 per month

Popular Areas:
Beeler Street

Squirrel Hill

Shadyside

Oakland

For Assistance Contact:
Community Housing Services
http://www.housing.cmu.edu/CommunityHousing

(412) 268-4990

ns1d@andrew.cmu.edu

Students Speak Out On...
Off-Campus Housing

"If you chose to leave campus housing after your freshman year, you should make sure you have a place to live for the rest of your time at CMU because getting back into campus housing is nearly impossible. There are some decent apartments close to campus if you don't like dorm life."

Q "They're a lot of places close to campus, and **rent is pretty cheap here.** The places are pretty nice for student housing."

Q "I would move out of a dorm after freshman year; **it is more refreshing and you can have a nice place.** Many students move into houses or apartments with friends. Rent is pretty cheap in Pittsburgh, so it's not hard to find a good place. Some people live as far as a fifteen-minute bus ride, but the buses are really good and come often, so it's not that bad."

Q "It is very convenient and **very much worth it** to live off cam-pus. You have to be careful where you choose to live, but the value is better and the community is less irritating."

Q "There is very convenient housing all over the place and around school. **It's much cheaper** than living in school dorms."

Q "**Commuting can be a pain.** Fraternities are essentially on campus and are a much better option."

Q "**Off-campus housing is extremely convenient.** There are a lot of apartments and houses nearby for rent; there has to be with so many students in the city. I live off campus, which is a beautiful twenty-two-minute walk for me. It's safe also. Usually first-year undergraduate students are required to live on-campus. I prefer that because you get to meet some great people when you have to live with them."

Q "Off-campus housing is pretty easy to find. **There are houses everywhere!** It's just a question of finding one that's close. I prefer to stay close to campus, and it can be hard getting a reasonable apartment close to campus. If you find people to live with, you can get into a house and that makes things much nicer and definitely cheaper."

Q "There are a lot of houses really close to the school, but they will probably be somewhat more expensive than on-campus housing. On the other hand, you will get a lot more space, but you will also probably have to pay for things like utilities. If you live a little farther from campus, you can still take the bus to school, and housing might be cheaper than on campus. **You will get a hell of a lot of more space.** You might want a car if you do that, since you might have a garage and free parking."

Q "Off-campus housing is easy. **There are nice residential neighborhoods** with lots of apartments available. Since the University of Pittsburgh pretty much adjoins our campus, landlords know that they will always have students who are looking for places to live."

Q "**Campus housing is very expensive.** Eventually— probably my junior year—I will be moving off campus. There are a bunch of apartments you can rent out. Housing offers apartments off-campus, which you might get into if you don't send in your housing payments on time. They are nice apartments and they are quieter, but you can switch into the dorms after the first semester if you want to. I like the apartments because I feel I have a nice separation from the school."

Q "Housing off campus is very convenient, and they are **all within walking distance.** If that's what you're going for (and I would), arrive earlier in the summer to get a place squared away. They do go quick. There are always people looking for roomies, though."

Q "Well, next year will be my second year living off-campus. After living off campus, **I could never imagine living on campus.** But for the first year or two, on-campus living is definitely the way to go. I know that's how I met most of my friends. But with off-campus housing, we have an entire house to ourselves, there's parking, and you don't have to deal with resident assistants and all that school stuff. You gain more responsibility with monthly rent and bills, too. I would highly recommend living off campus the last two years."

Q "It's very convenient, and I recommend it. Don't be one of those dorks that lives on campus in a dorm for his whole college career. **Get off campus ASAP.**"

The College Prowler Take On...
Off-Campus Housing

There's a large selection of houses and apartments to choose from in the nearby area. Most students love their off-campus residences, but the relationship between students and their houses is not without its pains. Having your own place is a great thing for a student, and dealing with things like paying bills, getting enough heat, trekking to campus, and even being wary of suspicious housemates is not enough to dampen the experience of having your own place. Students can find themselves spread out in Oakland, Shadyside, and Squirrel Hill, but most students renting houses end up living on nearby Beeler Street. The street itself is like a small community of CMU students living off campus. On the weekends, there's usually at least one party somewhere close by.

Finding off-campus space isn't much of a problem. The housing department makes it trouble-free to find and secure a location and provides students with information packets and many private listings only available to the CMU community. Unfortunately, you'll probably have to do at least ten minutes of walking to get to campus. This isn't so bad though, especially considering the impressive condition of many of the houses and apartments. If you can find an off-campus place that is well-maintained and is set up so that you don't have to pay for utilities (Pittsburgh has freezing winters), the move from campus to a nearby apartment or house is definitely worth it. If you can find a bunch of friends to live with and drive down rents, think about moving off campus by at least your junior year. Be careful though! Students warn that campus housing can be a disaster if you don't check out the place before you choose to rent it.

The College Prowler™ Grade on
Off-Campus Housing: A

A high grade in Off-Campus Housing indicates that apartments are of high quality, close to campus, affordable, and easy to secure.

Diversity

The Lowdown On...
Diversity

American Indian:
1%

Asian or Pacific Islander:
22%

African American:
4%

Hispanic:
5%

White:
43%

International:
11%

Unknown:
15%

Out of State:
70%

Most Popular Religions
There are a lot of Christian groups. Most religious activity takes place off-campus.

Political Activity
Most students are politically and socially liberal. Though the campus has its share of protests, students are generally not outspoken about their political views. Many consider the student body to be generally apathetic.

Gay Tolerance
The campus is very accepting of its gay students and has on-campus student groups such as SoHo, CMUout, ALLIES, and SafeZone. However, like most of CMU's student body, the sizable gay community is relatively quiet.

Economic Status
CMU has students from diverse economic backgrounds, but there seems to be a predominant amount with wealthy parents. Some students complain about all the "rich kids."

Minority Clubs
CMU's minority clubs are a noticeable social force on campus. The college offers a number of Asian and Indian clubs that throw parties and sponsor different events. There's also an African American fraternity, and Asian fraternity, and a Jewish fraternity.

Students Speak Out On...
Diversity

> **"The campus is more diverse than New York City. There is a large Asian population, several Indians, and then a bunch of others. It's really diverse, but people often stick with their own kind. Many come straight off the boats, so they feel like they need to stay with people like themselves."**

"**The campus is very diverse.** This is one area where the school really shines. Kids come from the U.S., Canada, Mexico, Asia, Europe, Africa . . . everywhere. There are all sorts of people with all sorts of interests. Unfortunately, I only get along with about ten to fifteen of them."

"I think the campus is **quite diverse.** The student population is, first of all, almost 25 percent Asian, and around 10 percent international (students from other countries). However, the male/female ratio is three to two or so; it's something like 70 percent male!"

"It's very diverse. I'm Asian, and I was born in Baltimore. My high school was 97 percent white, and here something like one-third is made up of 'minorities,' so it's very different. It's still nice, and p**eople are from all over the states and the world**. They all have different backgrounds; it's nice in that respect."

"It's very diverse. A lot of people are **fresh off the boat from other countries.** There are kids from all across the United States. There are not many black people or Hispanics, but we have a lot of white, Chinese, Japanese,

Indian, Korean, and Arab students. As in all colleges though, it's pretty segregated. The Asians stick with the Asians, the blacks with the blacks, the fruits with the fruits, the farm boys with the farm boys."

Q "The campus is very diverse, **maybe even too much** in my opinion"

Q "I feel like it's really diverse. I hear at least **three different languages** other than English every day."

Q "There are lots of people from eastern countries, but **very few African Americans.**"

Q "It's pretty diverse. **I feel like the minority being white.**"

Q "There are enormous amounts of diversity. There's a large Asian and Indian student body, but **no racial tension**. It's a very comfortable environment in that respect. One of the things I love about CMU is that you meet people from every place imaginable."

Q "There's next to **no African-Americans**, and we're high on Asians. There are lots of cultural groups out there if you want them."

Q "Well, there is a large international community, especially from Asia. Sometimes they can be very **cliquey and closed-minded,** but sometimes they add a little insight into other cultures."

Q "The diversity is quite good. There's a decent number of minorities and international students. **The male/female ratio could use some work, though.**"

Q "I think it is very diverse, not only ethnically, but also in interests. Sometimes everyone is so focused on their studies that it's difficult to take advantage of the diversity, but if you get involved in student activities, **you'll meet all sorts of people.**"

Q "I'd say CMU has a lot of Asians and Americans, but **there are actually not that many blacks.** It's kind of different for me, and I guess it's not as great as I would like it to be."

The College Prowler Take On...
Diversity

Carnegie Mellon prides itself on its diversity. The opportunity students have to meet people of different races, religions, and backgrounds is something that has a phenomenal impact on student life. Campus diversity gives a worldly experience to the students of a school isolated deep within Western Pennsylvania. As students claim, it never really feels like any race on campus is a majority (even though whites outnumber other races). The ethnic whirlwind that is CMU can be a bit dizzying at times. Because of the school's unprecedented diversity in some areas, it's easy to forget that there are some groups that aren't fairly represented, namely females. Carnegie Mellon's piteous male/female ratio is a major detractor to prospective students (as well as a constant downer for some male students). It's also true that the campus does not have a sizable African American or Hispanic population, especially when compared to the high concentration of other minorities. That said, the mélange of students at CMU is like nothing else most students have ever experienced.

Except for the dearth of women, all different races, religions, classes, and, geographic regions can be found in abundance on campus. As a student, CMU's diverse environment is a way to further your education by learning about the differences among people. If you're eager to learn about other cultures, Carnegie Mellon can provide a fantastic real-world education.

The College Prowler™ Grade on

Diversity: A-

A high grade in Diversity indicates that ethnic minorities and international students have a notable presence on campus, and that students of different economic backgrounds, religious beliefs, and sexual preferences are well-represented.

Guys & Girls

The Lowdown On...
Guys & Girls

Men Undergrads:	Women Undergrads:
61%	39%

Birth Control Available?

Yes. Female students who have had an exam with their home doctor or have an exam with Health Services can have their birth control prescriptions filled at health services for $10. Health Services offers all forms of birth control; pills, patches, and the shot. They also sell discounted condoms for $.25.

Dress Code

This is not a preppy school. Yes, some students do dress sharp, but the number of students wearing AMD Processor shirts is usually greater than the number of students wearing A+F. Most students don't have time to think about how they're going to dress and just roll out of bed and go to class unkempt. When it's time to party, however, the guys clean up and the girls spend time getting ready. Anything goes here. This school has trench coats, capes, jeans, and Prada. You'll even see your share of shorts in the middle of winter—even if it is thirty degrees out.

Social Scene:

Initiating interaction on campus is one of the greatest social hurdles CMU students have to face. Once students find their niche however it's not that bad. Poor social interaction is a downside that many students expect when coming to a school filled with introverted and focused young adults (nerds). There is really no social hierarchy on campus, and you can usually find a social butterfly for every kid who's socially awkward. The biggest challenge here is getting people to mix with others beyond their majors, colleges, or clubs.

Hookups or Relationships?

A lot of girls on campus are in relationships, but not always with CMU guys. There is a sizable pool of singles, however, and commitment-free hookups can be a common occurrence if you want them to be.

Best Place to Meet Guys/Girls:

Students are so involved in their studies and other activities that it's not surprising for guys and girls to hit it off while studying in the dorms, taking notes in class, or working on extracurricular activities. For students who don't want their romantic life to be too scholastic, there're some good house parties most weekends where singles go in hopes of meeting a significant other. Going to clubs and bars is a good way to meet non-CMU students who are out to have a little fun.

Important Note!

If you're looking to up your odds, you might have to wait to the end of the spring semester, when the number of "hotties" at CMU seems to flourish. This is the time when students trade their bulky coats for tank-tops and venture into the sun after months of being sealed in their dorm rooms and computer clusters. This is also the best time of the year to grab a blanket and go out to the middle of campus ("The Cut") in hopes of spotting some hot young women and studly young men tossing a football, listening to music, and maybe even having a few discrete drinks.

Did You Know?

Top Places to Find Hotties:

1.　　The Cut
2.　　The Frats
3.　　The Computer Clusters

Top Places to Hookup:

1.　　Frats
2.　　The football field
3.　　Empty classrooms
4.　　Flagstaff
5.　　Off-campus parties

Students Speak Out On...
Guys & Girls

"I believe it was Playboy who ranked CMU as one of the top ten ugliest campuses, but if you manage to get into the drama department, you'll find many hotties awaiting your arrival."

Q "**Everyone's really smart.** I've never met so many socially-inept people in my whole life. People are of average good looks in general, but it's tarnished by the fact that most students do not observe good hygiene."

Q "There are actually more guys than girls, so you think it'd be great for girls, but actually **people at CMU are really eclectic** and you may only be attracted to .0007 percent of the opposite sex. Come to CMU and see why. Actually, there is saying on campus, 'Sex kills. Come to CMU and live forever.'"

Q "Ha! **The girls leave much to be desired.** I don't know what it is, but CMU attracts a wholly undesirable kind of girl. I am so unsexed and bitter that I didn't pick a school with a better girl to guy ratio. I have no idea how the guys are. I suspect they'd be a catch because they're going to be very financially secure someday."

Q "**People are so geeky here**. I've heard some science majors refer to having sex as 'knitting genes.'"

Q "We're certainly **not the most attractive campus**, but it's not like there aren't any attractive people around. There's the University of Pittsburgh and a few other colleges around. The male to female ratio is three to two, but we're a nerd school; what do you expect? When you get out of here and you're starting off at about fifty or sixty grand a year, it'll all be worth it."

Q "During my freshman year in the computer science department, **there were more guys named David than there were girls, period.** I wouldn't say that the majority of the girls are 'hot,' but there are plenty of good lookers if you know where to go. You are better off 'sightseeing' down the street at the University of Pittsburgh. Usually, a lot of females from area colleges come by the fraternities on the weekends."

Q "Supposedly, Playboy magazine once rated CMU as the **second ugliest campus in the country**, except for the College of Fine Arts (CFA). That's not really true, but there are lots of funny-looking people (which I think makes the school interesting). The part about the CFA is true, however. I don't know how it happens, but the fine arts students are usually always good looking. I don't want to say this just because I'm a drama student, but the truth is our profession and area of study relies heavily on looks because the faculty wants us to be marketable in the professional world. Since we want to be successful actors, part of that includes what we look like. This, of course also applies to the musicians. So in general, either the students in CFA are hot, or they are cute, interesting, or have a marketable look."

Q "If you are looking for someone to date, try the College of Fine Arts first, even though there are others. Plus, the University of Pittsburgh adjoins our campus; with around 30,000 students, there is something for everyone! Of course, we all know that **looks aren't important.**"

Q "We are right next to the University of Pittsburgh, so even though the actual campus population may be lacking in good looks, there are always **good-looking people right next door.** The bar and club scene can be pretty active, but I am a computer science major, so I rarely have time for that. Usually, I am more into independent parties, and since I already have a girlfriend, I don't need to go clubbing."

○ "A lot of **people tend to stick to their own**. We have a lot of Indian or other Asian people, and they tend to hang out with only other Indians or Asians. The social scene on campus can be pretty depressing. For the most part, you will probably want to shop at Pitt for chicks. There are a few 'hotties' though, and if you are decent-looking where you live now, then your attractiveness multiplies by ten here just because most of the guys are tiny fat little nerds and chicks don't go for that. A lot of the women aren't much better. There are some good looking ones, but the majority isn't. It's depressing."

○ "I don't check out guys, but **girls are usually not hot.** Actually, believe it or not, it depends on the weather. You see, when it's cold and perhaps snowy, girls wear way too much clothes. That just takes all the sexiness away. Once summer comes it's like, 'Hey, this school is starting to get better.' What's also cool about the sunny days is that a lot of people chill outside and sit on the grass, or play sports. That's cool."

○ "The saying on campus for guys is, **'The odds are good, but the goods are odd.'** There are a lot of nerds, but the guys are generally decent and really nice. A lot of them sit in front of the computer playing games all day. I heard that Playboy chose our school as one of the ugliest schools for girls a couple of years ago. It's not that bad, though."

○ "You would think the guys would be hot considering the larger proportion of guys, but they're not. Well, I guess there are a few, but **they're most likely taken.** The guys that I made friends with are extremely nice. I haven't really met a jerk yet. The girls are girls, and it really depends on who you hang out with, I guess. I know I made a bunch of really good friends first semester, and now were living together next year!"

Q "**It's not that hot both ways.** There are lots of 'freaks and geeks,' including me. Attractive girls are in extremely short supply, but they have quite a choice due to the unbalanced male/female ratio."

Q "The guys are plentiful. You have a wide variety from the jocks, to the non-social computer nerds, to the artists, to everything. **The girls are becoming more plentiful,** and people are more attractive than the typical stereotype of CMU. Besides, both the boys and girls have strong money potential when they graduate."

Q "There are more guys than girls, so **girls have good odds.** However, there are a bunch of anti-social folks because they are always working on computers and engineering things."

Q "I heard once that this was actually **the second-most ugly campus in the country.** I don't believe this because of the lookers in the College of Fine Arts. The CFA kids are pretty hot, especially those in drama. This is one of the top drama schools in the country, and they want to produce talented people that have the look that's marketable for TV, stage, and film. You find a CFA guy or girl, and you're golden!"

The College Prowler Take On...
Guys & Girls

CMU students will unabashedly tell you that their campus is not an attractive one. It doesn't help the situation any that the cold weather forces guys and girls to stay bundled up in coats and jackets for most of the year. The lopsided male/female ratio is hard for both sexes, but especially for the guys. CFA students seem to be really proud of their looks. All the physical praise for CMU's artistic students isn't unfounded though; most of them are pretty fine. Many of the students studying less technical fields are actually pretty normal-looking. There are some students, though, who aren't too concerned about their looks or hygiene, and this is one of the reasons why the school has gotten such a bad reputation as a place to find hot guys and girls.

Students aren't coming to CMU looking for hotties. Due to the great disparity in gender, most girls would think their chances of finding a man are pretty good at CMU. However, most girls on campus have had to find consolation in the saying, "The odds are good, but the goods are odd." The situation for guys at CMU isn't as bad as some would think either. When you've exhausted the limited pool of CMU ladies, you can always outsource your romantic interests to Pitt, where the women are in abundance. Nonetheless, this is not the school for exploratory sexual exploits, though some students, especially those in CFA, have been known to get a little wild.

The College Prowler™ Grade on
Guys: C-

A high grade for Guys indicates that the male population on campus is attractive, smart, friendly, and engaging, and that the school has a decent ratio of guys to girls.

The College Prowler™ Grade on
Girls: D+

A high grade for Girls not only implies that the women on campus are attractive, smart, friendly, and engaging, but also that there is a fair ratio of girls to guys.

Athletics

The Lowdown On...
Athletics

Athletic Division:
NCAA Division III

Conference:
UAA

Men's Varsity Sports:
Basketball
Football
Golf
Cross Country
Track
Soccer
Swimming
Tennis

Women's Varsity Sports:
Basketball
Cross Country
Track
Soccer
Swimming
Tennis

Cheerleading

Volleyball

Club Sports:
Crew

Ultimate Frisbee

Baseball

Volleyball (Men's)

Lacrosse

Ice-Hockey

Fencing

Women's Softball

Water Polo

Badminton

Aussie Rules Football

Wrestling

Squash

Cycling

Explorers

Intramurals:
Badminton

Basketball

Bowling

Spades

Call Pool

Chess

Darts

Euchre

Floor Hockey

Foosball

Football

Indoor Soccer

Kickball

Pinochle

Racquetball

Soccer

Softball

Table Tennis

Tennis

Ultimate Frisbee

Volleyball

Water Basketball

Water Polo

Fields

Gesling Stadium
Intramural (IM) Field

School Mascot

Tartan

Colors

Scarlet and White

Getting Tickets

There's no need to get tickets to attend a CMU sporting event. Even at the most important football games, the bleachers are only spotted with spectators.

Most Popular Sports

On the varsity level, the football and soccer teams have the largest presence on campus, but that presence is still pretty small. All of the IM sports are very popular. Volleyball seems to have mass appeal across campus, and ultimate Frisbee and crew have their cult followings.

Overlooked Teams

The club baseball team has been trying to go varsity for a few years but has so far been unable to get the money from the University.

Best Place to Take a Walk

Schenley Park or Frick Park

Gyms/Facilities

Skibo Gym

Skibo Gym is the largest gym on campus, but due to its very poor conditions it's clearly not the best. Though the gym does boast an expansive free-weight collection, most of the weights are falling apart. The weight room is often too crowded on afternoons to accommodate the number of students looking to lift. The gym does feature several basketball courts, indoor tennis courts, all-purpose rooms, track equipment, and a fencing room. There's some cardio equipment, but half of that equipment is usually broken.

UC Gym

The UC Gym is a series of athletic facilities located within the University Center in the middle of campus. In addition to a small but well-kept weight-room, the gym also features an aerobics room (with classes taught regularly by faculty) and a cardio room. The most impressive features of the UC Gym are its popular basketball courts, five squash/racquetball courts, and a recreational swimming pool.

Outdoor Tennis Courts

These six beautiful outdoor courts are built into the ground and are lighted for nighttime play.

Students Speak Out On...
Athletics

"What varsity sports? If you love sitting in the bleachers with your friends and cheering on the football team, CMU is not for you. Intramural (IM) sports, on the other hand, are pretty popular and offer many different sports and leagues based on ability."

"**Do we have sports on campus?** I'm just joking, but that's how most of the student body feels. We are not an athletic school, and it's rare to hear anything about our football team. You can start any IM sports team you want. You can even play 'gaming,' that's when people play online computer games against each other. It's quite competitive on Sunday afternoons."

"What? **We play sports here?** You mean the chess team or the ping-pong club, right?"

"**Varsity sports aren't very big**; we're Division III. I think IM, on the other hand, is huge. I'd say about 75 percent of the campus plays some sort of IM sport."

"**IM sports are huge on campus.** A good majority of the students play one of the IM sports. There are a ton of them. Varsity sports aren't as big to watch compared to other schools."

"Do we have varsity sports? Seriously, sports like track and crew have a pretty good showing, but that isn't a reason to come here. **IM sports are pretty huge** if you can find a good group to enter them with."

Q "Sports are decent. We have a good football team, but **no one really watches them.** We are surprisingly good at a lot of stuff. IM is pretty big. I play just about everything on IM, and there are around fifty sports you can play. They go year-round, so no matter what, if you want to play sports you can."

Q "I wanted to try out for tennis, but didn't like the coach that much so I didn't try out. **Intramurals are pretty big.** I imagine it's because most people want to devote most of their time to studying, so intramurals is convenient for them."

Q "Varsity sports aren't that big to people. A lot of **people are too into studying and work to support the athletics.** I play football, but I had more people at my high school games. A lot of people play IM, though. They have a lot of sports, and a lot of people participate."

Q "IM is much bigger than varsity. **CMU is hardly a school for jocks,** but it is good for people that just want to have some fun. There's some nice competition. There's even a golf course basically on campus."

Q "Well, it's a Division III school. There's support for the varsity and club sports, but it's **not an overwhelming spirit.**"

Q "Varsity sports are doing really well. **I'm on the swim team, and we just placed fourth in the nation**. I know a lot of athletes, and it's a great group to be in. Almost everyone I know is in at least one IM sport. There are a ton of them to join. I was in six, I think."

The College Prowler Take On...
Athletics

Varsity sports may feature competitive play, but their popularity falls short when compared to the enormous success of intramural sports on campus. Though neglected by students, Carnegie Mellon's Division III sports are still important to the athletes that play them. CMU competes against Emory, NYU, Wash U, Case Western, and Brandeis, among schools in the University Athletic Association. The large number of students involved in IM sports is shocking to some considering the school's un-athletic reputation. The Frisbee and crew club teams have a devoted following, and provide a social atmosphere for their participants. Playing these sports is a fun and lighthearted way for most students to stay in shape in between studying.

Athletics events on campus are only important to the athletes involved in them. If you've always dreamed of coming to a college where you could cheer the football team to victory every weekend, you need to go down the street about a half mile to the University of Pittsburgh. The best way to experience the excitement and competition of sports is to create it yourself. Sign up for your own IM team, give it a crazy name, and when the referee calls you for a foul, curse him out like it's game seven of the NBA Finals.

The College Prowler™ Grade on

Athletics: C

A high grade in athletics indicates that students have school spirit, that sports programs are respected, that games are well-attended, and that intramurals are a prominent part of student life.

Nightlife

The Lowdown On...
Nightlife

Club and Bar Prowler: Popular Nightlife Spots!

Déjà Vu Lounge

620 Penn Ave, Strip District
(412) 263-2877
www.dejavuloungepa.com

Déjà Vu is a nice place to relax and unwind during the evenings but can get pretty packed at night. It's a lounge/ club with different rooms that play a mix of techno and Top 40. Drinks are probably the most expensive in the city, the dress code is not that strict either. Many people go here first since there is no cover and then head down the block to Sanctuary later in the night. You must be twenty-one to get in, and IDs are not checked that hard.

Friday & Saturday: Sushi & Martini Happy Hour.

Club Lite (Formerly Donzi's)

1501 Smallman Street
Boardwalk Complex, Strip District
(412) 281-1585

Lite makes up half of the

➡

infamous "Boardwalk" in the Strip District. There are quite few a clubs in this area, but Donzi's/Lite has been there since 1991 while the others come and go pretty fast. You must be twenty-one to get into Lite and you must be dressed properly. They don't allow hats, throwbacks, tucked-in sweater, doo-rags, or army wear. Parking is usually around $5 and is right outside of the club.

Specials:

Wednesday: "Wild Wednesdays College Night." $1 Drinks till Midnight, $5 cover charge; Hip Hop, Techno, Top 40

Friday: "The Friday Night Dance Party." $1 Drinks till Midnight, $7 cover charge

Saturday: "Top 40 Night." Free drinks for anyone wearing skirt & high heels between 10-11 p.m.; $7 cover charge

Matrix, The

1 Station Square Unit E7, Station Square

(412) 261-2220

Occupancy: 1,000

The Matrix combines four different rooms into one night club. Club Liquid plays Miami-style trance, Club Exit plays New York-style house, Club Goddess plays Top 40 music and corny old-school hip hop, and Club Velvet plays Latin music that is slightly old. The Matrix is a really nice club, and gets very packed, but they have a dress code. The best day to hit up the Matrix is with-

out a doubt on Thursday.
Specials:

Tuesday: "Service Industry Night." $0.75 drinks until midnight; $5 cover charge

Thrusday: "Thursday X." $1 Drinks till midnight, $5 cover charge

Friday: "Friday Fusion." $1.50 Drinks till 10 p.m., $8 cover charge

Saturday: $1.50 Drinks till 11 p.m., $8 cover charge

Sanctuary

620 Penn Avenue, Strip District

(412) 263-2877

Sanctuary is an upscale dance club that plays everything from 50 Cent to Madonna's "Just Like a Prayer." This club used to be a church, but they renovated it to make it really nice inside. Waitresses are dressed up as Catholic school girls. The people usually dress nicer here than in other clubs in Pittsburgh, and drinks are more expensive as well. Don't expect to find any drink specials or wild college kids here. There's a strict dress code, and you must be twenty-one. Fridays and Saturdays are the best nights to go.
Specials:

Mondays: "Midnight Mass" $2 drinks till midnight, $5 cover charge

Friday & Saturday: Open, no specials, but gets very packed

Tequila Willies

1501 Smallman Street

Boardwalk Complex, Strip District

(412) 281-1585

Occupancy: 600

TW's makes up the other half of the "Boardwalk" and is relatively new. Same type of Dress Code as Lite. You pay one cover to get into the Boardwalk and have access to both Tequila Willies and Lite. You must be twenty-one to get in and they scan IDs at the door to make sure they are real. The best night to hit up Lite and TW's is on Wednesday.

Specials:

Wednesday: "Coyote Ugly College Night." $1 Drinks till midnight, $5 cover charge; Top 40

Friday: "X-treme Fridays." $7 cover charge

Saturday: "South of the Border Saturdays." $7 cover charge

Mad Mex

370 Atwood St., Oakland

(412) 681-5656

The place to go for giant margaritas and Mexican food. Thanks to popular student specials and happy hours, the place is usually packed with both Pitt and CMU kids. On Fridays, many students come here to start their weekend at 4 p.m., when margaritas and beers are half-off until 6 p.m. Things get even more packed later in the evening. From 10 p.m.-11 p.m., giant margaritas are $5, and after 11 p.m., all food is half-off. No one leaves here sober.

Panther Hollow Inn (PHI)

4611 Forbes Ave., Oakland/ CMU

(412) 682-9999

This bar is CMU tradition, although you won't read about it in any brochures. Thursday nights at PHI are packed with CMU students taking advantage of $4 pitchers. It's a couple of steps away from the dorms, right on Forbes.

Peter's Pub

116 Oakland Ave., Oakland

(412) 681-7465

Peter's is a club on the University of Pittsburgh's campus located in the heart of Oakland. It's a college hangout with mostly Pitt kids, but the CMU students that know what's up come down here for fun. Thursday is often the best night with $3 pitchers until midnight. Monday is great. You can dance to the latest hip-hop upstairs and rub shoulders with the Pitt football and basketball teams.

Pittsburgh Deli Company
(PDC, The Deli)

728 Copeland St., Shadyside

(412) 682-DELI

PDC is another local bar within a short hike from campus. Located right off of Walnut

Street, this eclectic restaurant/bar offers live music throughout the week as well as half price food after 9 p.m. It's the closest thing Yuppie-style Shadyside has to a hippie bar.

Shady Grove

5500 Walnut St., Shadyside

(412) 697-0909

A relatively new bar, this local hotspot is arguably one of the most popular places in Shadyside. Known for its trendy New York-style décor and a busy (and often loud) atmosphere, many students come here for beer specials as well as frozen margaritas and daiquiris. Right upstairs is the site of the Walnut Grill, a slightly more low-key room. Come up here to sip martinis. Stay downstairs if you want darts.

Other Places to Check Out:

Touch

Bash

Chemistry

Pub IG

Mardi Gras

Shadyside Saloon

Club Havana

Cumpie's

Bar 11

Mario's

Shootz Café

Lava Lounge

Tiki Bar

Dowe's

Dee's

Bossa Nova

Sports Rock

Buffalo Blues

What to Do if You're Not 21:

Club Laga

3609 Forbes Ave (4th Floor)

Oakland

412-682-2050

Club Laga has been open for around six years, which is pretty good for Pittsburgh since most clubs go out of business in a few years. Not only can you come here to dance the night away and bump heads with other college kids in the area, but you can also catch acts from groups such as Wu Tang to local groups such as the Clarks. To get into Laga, you must to be eighteen and have a college ID.

Fridays: "Groove," $10 Cover Charge, open till 4 a.m.

Saturday: "Hip-Hop Party," $5 cover charge before midnight, $10 after, open till 3:30 a.m.

Rock Jungle

5 Station Square East

Station Square

412-765-2200

Located in between Hooter's and the Matrix in Station Square, Rock Jungle used to be a 21-and-over club, but has now transformed into an 18-and-over venue, that plays Top 40 and popular hip-hop. Proper dress code is required.

Fridays: "The Grind" $10
Cover: $2 drinks 9-11p.m.

Saturdays: $8 Cover Charge,
Must be under twenty-one

Sundays: $8 Cover Charge,
Must be under twenty-one

House Parties:

House parties are big at CMU.
You can find many parties
going on every weekend at
Roselawn Apartments or on
Beeler Street. The trick is to
ask around and get on an
e-mail list that can give you
weekly updates on all the lat-
est events. Some CMU house
parties charge a small cover
(around $3) since they provide
you with beer and a cup.

Organization Parties

Many clubs at CMU will often
rent out a restaurant or night
club and throw private parties.
These parties are usually a lot of
fun and are thrown by groups
such as Spirit, Architecture,
Design, Asian Student Association, Korean Student Association, and the Indian Student
Association. Look for these
organizations to partner with
similar ones at the University
of Pittsburgh. These parties are
usually a lot better.

Student Favorites

PHI
Shady Grove
Tequila Willies
Matrix
Déjà Vu Lounge

Useful Resources for Nightlife

http://www.barsmart.com

http://www.pghnightlife.com

Pittsburgh City Paper

Local Specialties

Iron City

Yuengling

Rolling Rock

Primary Areas with Nightlife:

Oakland
Shadyside
Southside
Strip District
Station Square
The Waterfront

Cheapest Place to Get a Drink:

P.H.I. (Panther Hollow Inn)

Favorite Drinking Games:

Kings
Beer Pong
Card Games
Century Club
Quarters
Power Hour

Students Speak Out On...
Nightlife

"If you're coming to CMU for the parties and the bars, you may be thinking of Central Michigan University. That's the wrong CMU. During freshmen year, frat parties are the big thing. After that, you'll probably be going to a lot of house parties."

Q "Also, several majors or departments throw their own parties. There are art parties, design parties, drama parties, and Frisbee parties. **People go to PHI bar.** For how popular it is, you'd think it's the only bar in Pittsburgh. It's real close to campus."

Q "I went to Rock Jungle twice and it was a disaster. **It was filled with skeezy old men with bad cologne** and gold chains trying to pick up eighteen-year-old girls"

Q "Parties take place on the edges of campus and consist of **small, dull house parties which would be too tame for most people's parents.** Do not believe the hype—college is not like the movies. It's depressing how lame college kids can be. CMU is not the place to party, and U. Pitt is a little too rugged for your average CMU student. Get ready for four years of frustrating parties where your grandma is more hip than the average student. Clubs and bars are plentiful if you have a fake ID, which most people do. Work hard and play hard I guess."

Q "Unlike New York, **there aren't very many bars and clubs for people under twenty-one.** There are a few places that have eighteen-and-over nights on certain days of the week. However, Pittsburgh is a smaller and more family-oriented city, so late night spots aren't that prominent."

Q "Pittsburgh **doesn't have the greatest nightlife,** but they do have some kicking bars, especially on the Southside and in the Strip. Shootz, Mario's, and Peter's Pub are all good places to go. You really can't go wrong if you want to go to a bar and you're on the Southside. The Strip has more clubs and that kind of scene."

Q "I'm not the most outgoing guy, but I've gone to Panama Jack's, which is a club that used to be close to campus. It wasn't too big or that great, but **it wasn't that bad** either, especially after a few drinks. There's also Rock Jungle, which is a blast."

Q "I've been to one bar since I've been at CMU because I turned twenty-one a month ago. You have to be twenty-one to get into all bars (**Pennsylvania has a very strict liquor law**). There are plenty of them in Pittsburgh. Between Oakland, the Southside, the Strip District and Downtown, there are many choices. I'm not into the club scene. The only ones that I know of are Rock Jungle in Station Square and Club Laga in Oakland. I've been to Laga for several concerts. We get some pretty good bands for cheap."

Q "I haven't been to many bars or clubs, but my friends have. I know of one in station square called Rock Jungle, it's easy to get to. **There's also a gay club in downtown called Pegasus.** As far as bars go, there's a whole bunch. Just to let you know, there isn't anything in downtown except for some clubs, bars, and the symphony. It's like a ghost town at night, but there are things to do in Oakland, which is where CMU is."

Q "Off campus, **there are a bunch of bars in Oakland**. The typical CMU bar, where most CMU kids go, is PHI. They have some pretty good beer specials on certain days of the week. The Southside also has a ton of bars, but they're mostly full of Pitt and Duquesne students. The Strip District boasts the most clubs. Try the Matrix on

Fridays, Sanctuary on Saturdays, and on Thursdays, go to PHI!"

Q "For those twenty-one and under, you can go to clubs in Oakland, down the block from CMU. Try Panama Jacks or Laga. You will find a mix of local Pittsburghers as well as CMU, and Pitt students there. **These clubs can get pretty packed,** but they don't serve alcohol unless you have an ID. There is also Rock Jungle in Station Square, which is really nice and big inside, but requires a cab ride! Try Rock Jungle on Sunday night.to PHI!"

Q "There is one bar in particular that CMU students go to because of its proximity to campus and because it's also inexpensive—PHI. **The club scene, if you have a good fake or are twenty-one, is all right.** I'm from New Jersey, so it's nothing like New York City, but it's livable. For your first year, you'll probably do the frat scene, which is definitely fun as an underclassman, but will get old as the years go by."

The College Prowler Take On...
Nightlife

As students get older, their opportunities to experience good nightlife also grows. As freshmen, most students only venture so far as the frat quad. By sophomore year, most students know friends with houses, and there's the opportunity for a lot of off-campus parties. By junior and senior year, most students have turned twenty-one and are ready to go explore the Pittsburgh club scene. Students can hit this scene even earlier if they bring a fake ID with them to college. If CMU has an official bar, it's the always-packed PHI (Panther Hollow Inn) on Forbes Avenue. Students patronize the bar on all nights of the week, and it's not impossible to sneak in if you're under twenty-one. The bar isn't the classiest place, though. It's kind of cramped, but students keep coming back.

Until you hit 21, most of the area's nightclubs will be pretty much off-limits. The frat scene is always an option for girls interested in basement dancing and beer pong. Parties on campus are very segregated. At CMU, fraternities and sororities aren't the only groups that throw exclusive parties. Most of the time if you go to a party, it is probably being thrown by some specific campus group or major. This is especially true for the students in the College of Fine Arts. It's just as common to hear someone talk about going to an art, architecture, design, or drama party as it is to hear someone talk about going to a frat party. There aren't a ton of house parties, but there are enough that students should have something to do every weekend.

The College Prowler™ Grade on

Nightlife: B-

A high grade in Nightlife indicates that there are many bars and clubs in the area that are easily accessible and affordable. Other determining factors include the number of options for the under-21 crowd and the prevalence of house parties.

Greek Life

The Lowdown On...
Greek Life

Number of Fraternities:
13

Number of Sororities:
13

Percent of Undergrad Men in Fraternities:
15%

Percent of Undergrad Women in Sororities:
11%

Frats on Campus:
Alpha Epsilon Phi
Beta Theta Phi
Delta Tau Delta
Delta Upsilon
Kappa Delta Rho
Kappa Sigma
Pi Kappa Alpha
Sigma Alpha Epsilon
Sigma Phi Epsilon
Sigma Tau Gamma
Sigma Nu
Theta Xi

→

Sororities on Campus:

Kappa Kappa Gamma
Zeta Psi Sigma
Delta Delta Delta
Kappa Alpha Theta
Delta Gamma

Other Greek Organizations

Kappa Phi Lambda
Lambda Phi Epsilon
Pi Delta Psi
Greek Council
Greek Peer Advisors
Interfraternity Council
Order of Omega
Panhellenic Council

Did You Know?

Once a year, the fraternities and sororities participate in a musical competition called Greek Sing.

Students Speak Out On...
Greek Life

> "The only parties that are on campus are held at the frats. They usually have a pretty good turnout. If dancing in a sweaty, humid room isn't your thing, then you are out of luck."

Q "I've been to some pretty fun frat parties. **The quality of frat guys depends very much on the fraternity.** Everyone I knew in Sigma Nu and Kappa Delta Roh were so nice. The Delta Tau Delta boys were jerks."

Q "I'd rather not spend my time talking about Greek life. **It's lame.**"

Q "**Greek life is a simple excuse for frat boys to prey on inexperienced college girls** who just want to dance. If you desire sex and male friendship so bad that you will pay dues for it, then you were born to be in a frat. If you have any dignity and respect, a sense of individuality, and intelligence, you will stay away from a frat. The sorority girls are just lame and not hot."

Q "**Well, it's a nerd school.** Most of us are too busy doing work to party every weekend, but we do have our frats and whatnot. There is Carnival, though. It's a three-day weekend dedicated to partying that's hosted by the school; we deserve it."

Q "About 15 percent of the students are in the Greek system. **I wouldn't say that they dominate,** but there are always plenty of parties outside of the frats and over at Pitt. People who work hard usually like to party hard, as well, and that's my real take on that. The scene is good if you want it to be."

Q "Fraternity life has helped make me a good event programmer and leader. **It's really expanded my social horizons** and forced me to meet lots of wonderful people. Even though the guys that I first came to school with have mostly graduated, I have a huge network of friends that will probably remain strong throughout the years."

Q "I'm in a fraternity, Alpha Epsilon Pi. There are 12 fraternities and five sororities here. **They tend to dominate most of the social scene, especially for freshmen.** We party a lot on Fridays and Saturdays during the first few weeks. About 15 percent of the campus goes Greek."

Q "**It is a strong component but not an essential one.** You are never pressured to participate, but you are always welcome. Usually, the frats and sororities have weekend parties, but because academics here are so important, there are very rarely parties during the week. They are all usually involved with charitable organizations and service, and are a positive influence on the school."

Q "I came from the University of Florida, so **the Greek life sucks** in comparison. There are a fair number of frats and sororities here, but personally, I am not a frat guy, and I don't like a lot of the guys in them. They serve cheap beer, they smoke bad pot, and all they really want to do is get the virgins drunk and into bed. Some are okay, but they are mostly lame, and the sad part is they don't even know it. I get along just fine without the frats. They don't really dominate the social scene, but they certainly are a big part of it. There are other parties all the time besides theirs, so if you aren't into cheesy frats, you can find other stuff."

Q "**It's not that great, in my opinion**, although some are good. I'll tell you that it depends on which ones girls think are good—they'll go there."

Q "I would say it doesn't dominate the social scene, but then again, I'm not in a frat. Probably most people in frats would say it dominates the social scene, so I don't know. I've hung out in some of their parties, **they're okay**, but they're not the best. The hygiene really sucks sometimes."

Q "**Our Greek life is pretty small.** It definitely does not dominate the social scene because there are a lot of parties that are non-Greek oriented. From experience, frats are fun the first week of school; that's about it."

Q "There's a pretty visible Greek community and **it's very popular on campus.** It's definitely not necessary to find a group of cool friends or be in the party scene, though. I'm not Greek, and I get along great."

Q "Have you ever seen Animal House? It's nothing like that. **The frats do not dominate.** There are plenty more things to do, but I guess it depends if you like going to frat parties or not. I'm not a huge fan, but sometimes they can be fun."

The College Prowler Take On...
Greek Life

Most outsiders are a little cautious of Greek life, but fraternity and sorority members share a proud allegiance to their organizations. The social scene at Carnegie Mellon is different from most other colleges. While it's true that frat parties make up a large percentage of the partying that takes place on and off campus, these events are never really big deals for non-Greek students. The influence that fraternities have on non-Greek students is a passive one, but the frat scene is popular for freshmen to explore even if they don't join. With the Morewood Gardens, New House, and Mudge dorms right next to the frat quad, freshmen have easy access to Panhellenic debauchery.

Students interested in the brotherhood or sisterhood that Greek life offers can find it at CMU. Orientation week is a good time to frequent frat parties and find out if going Greek is something you'd be interested in. Only 15 percent of students go Greek, so there's really no pressure to join, and it does not signal the end of your social life at CMU. The sororities don't really throw any parties, but naturally, girls can go to whatever frat party they want, no questions asked. A number of Pitt girls actually come up to CMU because the frats are cleaner and safer than the ones at U. Pitt. Guys who aren't brothers may have a little more trouble getting in, but it's not impossible especially if you have friends who can get you on the guest list.

The College Prowler™ Grade on

Greek Life: C+

A high grade in Greek Life indicates that sororities and fraternities are not only present, but also active on campus. Other determining factors include the variety of houses available and the respect the Greek community receives from the rest of the campus.

Drug Scene

The Lowdown On...
Drug Scene

Most Prevalent Drugs on Campus:

Alcohol

Marijuana

Caffeine

Ritalin

Adderall

Liquor-Related Referrals:

0

Liquor-Related Arrests:

38

Drug-Related Referrals:

0

Drug-Related Arrests:

1

Drug Counseling Programs

The Counseling and Student Development Center

Phone: (412) 268-2922

Services: alcohol assessment services, short-term counseling, support for children of alcoholics, alcohol related literature

The Office of Student Affairs

Phone: (412) 268-2075

Services: educational programming for groups/organization, alcohol related films and literature

Student Health Services

Phone: (412) 268-2157

Services: alcohol dependency assessments, evaluation of alcohol on physical well-being

The Health Educator, Nancy Schmidt

Phone: (412) 268-7888

Services: one-on-one counseling, educational programming for groups/organizations

Interfaith Counsel

Phone: (412) 621-8875

Services: religious pastoral counseling and pastoral care

Employee Assistance Program (LifeWorks)

Phone: 1-888-267-8126

Services: alcohol assessment services, short-term counseling and referral services

Students Speak Out On...
Drug Scene

{ **"Carnegie Mellon University doesn't have a lot of drugs. But if you're looking for drugs, the best place to go would probably be the frats."**

Q **"I don't think that many kids at CMU use drugs**, but the ones who do have enough money to hit the scene hard."

Q **"You have to look hard for drugs.** I haven't encountered people doing them. People drink, but drugs are not big. Go to Pitt for that kind of thing. They know about drugs."

Q **"It's a pretty mild drug scene.** If you're desperate enough for drugs then you'll find them."

Q "Same as anywhere, **you can find it** if you know the right people."

Q **"Marijuana is probably the most widely-used drug**, but I don't know much about it because I don't smoke. I don't like it. I know a few people who get a hold of stuff, but overall, substance abuse is relatively minor because people are smart here and know how to control what they do, whatever it is."

Q **"My friends got cited for smoking pot** and had to go to drug abuse meetings. The punishment was way too strict and the police were jerks."

Q "If you look hard enough, **you can find whatever your heart desires.** I'd start with the frats. I'm not saying we're all a bunch of druggies, but it is college, and everyone experiments on those cold winter nights. I mean, what else are you going to do? It's too cold to step outside."

Q "You can get it all at CMU if you know where to go. Drugs are bad though, and you should stay away from them. I know a ton of students that pretty much ruined their CMU education because of substance abuse. As far as peer pressure is concerned, you won't find that at CMU. **Drugs are usually prominent in the drama department.** I guess it's so that the actors and actresses can act better."

Q "It's there, but **it's not rampant.** The only drug use I personally encountered was people out in the dark smoking pot. You can certainly avoid it if you want to."

Q "I had an awful roommate in the beginning of the year. He did every drug imaginable. I think that a lot of colleges have their problems with drugs, but **there's not a big one at CMU.**"

Q "You can get your hands on just about anything; **lots of people smoke weed.**"

Q "I don't know; I don't hear people talking much about that. I think that if there are drugs, **people don't make such a big deal about it**, or maybe not many people do it. I don't think many people do it, but then again, I don't go around asking."

Q "I've heard a story about this guy who smoked pot all day without even going to school. He did it so much that **his room was always filled with smoke like a cave or something**. Oh, what happened to him? He got kicked out, of course."

The College Prowler Take On...
Drug Scene

You need to look pretty hard to find drug activity on campus. It always seems like students know of someone who's really into drugs, but no students themselves ever admit to descending into drug use. There is some noticeable use of softer drugs, however. Alcohol seems to be the drug of choice for most students and just about everyone knows that guy who sits in his room and smokes pot all day. Non-users feel very little pressure to indulge in drugs.

CMU has less drug-use than your average high school. It's true that students sometimes freak out before a test, and begin to fiend for caffeine. There are also rumors of Ritalin use, but like most drug use on campus, no one ever really admits to seeing it happen. Drugs are not a dominant force in CMU culture, even though it isn't that hard to attain them.

The College Prowler™ Grade on
Drug Scene: B

A high grade in the Drug Scene indicates that drugs are not a noticeable part of campus life; drug use is not visible, and no pressure to use them seems to exist.

Campus
Strictness

The Lowdown On...
Campus Strictness

What Are You Most Likely to Get Caught Doing on Campus?

- Drinking underage
- Public urination or indecency
- Parking illegally
- Making too much noise in your dorm
- Downloading copyrighted materials
- Sending unsolicited e-mail (spam)
- Bringing food or drink in a cluster
- Running around on roof tops of buildings
- Having candles and incense sticks in your dorm
- Running stop signs
- Streaking on the field
- Not having a wristband for the gyms

Students Speak Out On...
Campus Strictness

"They're not at all strict unless you're being stupid. Your dorm room is your sanctuary. You can pretty much do whatever you want in there and it's your own business. Campus police only get involved when your neighbors start complaining."

Q "If you get caught with alcohol and are underage, **you will be cited.** But that is the case with almost anywhere you go. Drugs are not tolerated either."

Q "**The police are very hardcore about drugs** but not drinking. I've walked past CMU police drunk and carried people who've been passed out, and they just looked the other way."

Q "The campus police have this great policy where you have immunity if you're caught drunk as long as you're helping the other person you are with. Plus, **the school is real light on substance abuse penalties and so on.** Although the drug scene barely exists, it has plenty of room to thrive."

Q "Usually, if you have a **'drug-related emergency,'** campus police will get you to a hospital without asking any questions."

Q "I think that the **campus police are not that strict about drugs.** Most people don't smoke in any buildings because it's not allowed and they abide by the rules, but with drinking, they aren't too strict unless it's underage."

Q "They can be strict, but for the most part, **they turn a blind eye** unless someone complains. There are frat parties on campus and they aren't raided unless the police have reason to believe something is going on."

Q "You aren't supposed to drink in campus housing if you're underage, and drugs, of course, are illegal. **I know that people still do that stuff and get away with it**, but not always. Usually, underage drinking is caught at the fraternities and the frats are the ones that usually get in trouble."

Q "**Don't get caught if you are underage.** They really are concerned about your safety, so if you are hurting, they will take you to the hospital and not get all on your case. But really, don't get caught."

Q "I'm not very sure about drugs, although I don't think they're allowed. I forgot because **it's rare to find drug problems** . . . maybe that's just what I think. Drinking is completely prohibited unless you are over the age of twenty-one. There have been about five cases of problems involving alcohol consumption only on my dorm floor. But I'm sure that there is much more illegal drinking going on everywhere on campus, not that campus police will be able to catch it all—unless there's a rat on the floor that is willing to report every illegal behavior of floor mates he sees."

Q "They're not as strict as one would think. There is some kind of amnesty thing they have that if students call for help for themselves or their friends because of intoxication, they don't get charged. People get internal citations sometimes for disorderly conduct due to drinking, but I don't know anyone who has been arrested for underage drinking, just reprimanded. I think they are strict with drugs, but I think **some are considered worse than others.** I did have a friend who spent a night in jail for marijuana possession, but I don't think he was caught on campus. A fraternity got in trouble for drug use or possession of some kind and their house was taken away for a year, but they are getting it back."

Q "The cops are cool with lots of things as long as you're not obnoxious about it. **They'll stand outside of the frats on weekends** when parties are going on and talk to people. They just want to make sure people are okay and get home safe"

Q "**The police don't bother any parties beyond warnings about noise,** and even those are rare. They also aren't allowed to enter the fraternities on campus for no reason, so that's nice. If you're caught for anything, I don't think they'll press any real charges; everything's internal. Plenty of people smoke around campus and don't get caught. As long as you're not stupid, you're fine."

Q "CMU has made this agreement I guess with Pittsburgh police. Basically, let's say that you're out one night and your friend gets really trashed. **CMU made it possible for students to call campus police without any fear of getting into major trouble.** The most that can happen to you is that you will get a fine. CMU does this just to ensure safety."

The College Prowler Take On...
Campus Strictness

The students say it best! The campus police really care about their safety. Students involved in drinking on and around campus never have a reason to be paranoid of getting a citation unless they're acting really stupid. Close your dorm room door and you and your friends can get plastered and bounce off the walls all night. So long as things are kept quiet and no one sees anything, there won't be any problems from authority. The police are here to protect students, not to bust them.

The campus realizes that most CMU students are mature and lets them enjoy their freedom. The drug and party scenes aren't too large and they never really get out of control, so the police don't have much to worry about in the first place. Even though students don't have much to fear from authorities, they shouldn't try to test their patience either.

The College Prowler™ Grade on

Campus Strictness: A

A high Campus Strictness grade implies an overall lenient atmosphere; police and RAs are fairly tolerant, and the administration's rules are flexible.

Parking

The Lowdown On...
Parking

Approximate Parking Permit Cost:
$510-1,320 per year

CMU Parking Services
(412) 268-2052
parking@andrew.cmu.edu
www.cmu.edu/ba/parking

Common Parking Tickets:
Expired Meter: $30
No Parking Zone: $40
Handicapped Zone: $200
Fire Lane: $100

Student Parking Lot?
Yes

Freshman Allowed to Park?
No

→

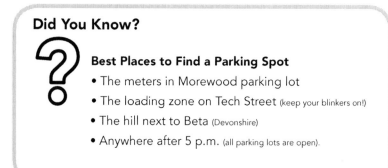

Did You Know?

Best Places to Find a Parking Spot

- The meters in Morewood parking lot
- The loading zone on Tech Street (keep your blinkers on!)
- The hill next to Beta (Devonshire)
- Anywhere after 5 p.m. (all parking lots are open).

Good Luck Getting a Parking Spot Here!

Margaret Morrison Street

The Boot!

If you accumulate three or more parking tickets, you better watch out! Your car will get this nice bright orange lock on your wheel.

Parking Permits

Faculty and grad students get priority selection for parking permits. It's very rare for undergrads to obtain a parking permit. Due to the overwhelming demand, you must apply for a parking permit and get put in the lottery drawing to obtain a spot.

Students Speak Out On...
Parking

"Parking here is tough because it's a relatively urban campus and all the teachers who commute also need spots. Usually, parking gets easier as the day goes on. All parking costs money until 6 p.m., after which it is free."

"**There is very little parking on campus.** If you are lucky enough to get a parking permit, you have to pay between $500 and $1,000 per year for it. You are better off just riding the bus."

"They only have one parking garage that's too small and it costs like a million dollars a year to park there. Most of the people I know who have cars **can't afford to drive** them to school."

"They really don't advise you to bring a car to school. It's a pretty bad situation. **Don't bring a car!** If you need to, you can apply for a campus parking pass, but good luck getting one. If you live off campus, you can apply for a city parking permit and park in specific zones. Bring a bike! It's free, you get exercise and you can park it anywhere; there are bike racks all over. Plus, it will allow you to explore the city in places that the bus can't take you and are too far to walk."

"**Parking? Where?** I think last year I must have gotten about ten tickets for parking, and my car has been towed once. In other words, parking on campus is a pain."

Q "Parking is strict. It is difficult to park on campus, and permits are super-expensive. I would say **don't have a car during your first year.** Throughout the residential areas in Pittsburgh, it's permit parking. So some people buy permits off of people so that they can park on one of the streets near campus. The permits for residents are only $20, but since they are in high demand, people have sold them for over $400."

Q "We get **free bus transportation** anywhere in the city with our student ID cards, so a car is not really necessary. I didn't have one my first two years here. I finally brought one this year, but I don't use it that often—just for going to the grocery store or driving home to Indianapolis for breaks. I've been here for four weeks and have not even used half a tank of gas!"

Q "Parking on campus sucks. **Let me reiterate, it's terrible.** There is little parking, and it's anywhere from $500 to $2,000 dollars to get a parking pass. I live just off campus where there is street parking for $20 if you live in the area. If you live on campus, I do not suggest bringing a car because they do ticket and the fines add up."

Q "If you have a car, you usually have to pay monthly or yearly in order to get parking space, and it's pretty expensive. **There's not much need to have a car, though,** because on-campus housing (which is enforced for the first year) is really close to school and things aren't usually so far. The tuition includes a bus sticker, which lets you ride the bus for free inside Pittsburgh. If you can afford a car (and parking) and aren't afraid of driving it in the snow, then bring a car."

The College Prowler Take On...
Parking

Parking for students is not convenient, and bringing a car is not necessary. To achieve a campus parking permit you'll have to be chosen in a lottery and even then, you'll have to fork over a lot of money to end up parking a car you probably won't need to use all that much. Students also have trouble parking on the city streets surrounding campus, as spots are rarely available, but those renting a house have the option to purchase a city parking permit for about $20—this works out well, since the only students who really need cars are the ones who would use them to commute to campus. Freshmen can't have cars on campus, so it's not really an issue for first-year students.

Due to all the parking problems, having a car on campus is more of a burden than anything else. Most students enjoy walking around campus. Fortunately, there's no pressure to bring a car so if you don't have the nicest whip don't worry. You can just leave that '88 Mercury Tracer at home.

The College Prowler™ Grade on
Parking: D-

A high grade in this section indicates that parking is both available and affordable, and that parking enforcement isn't overly severe.

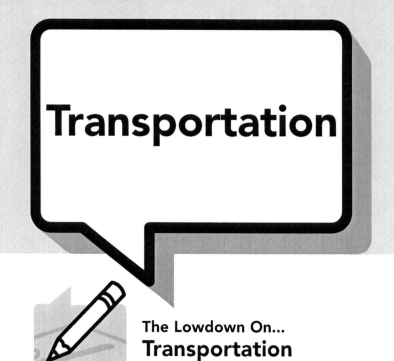

Transportation

The Lowdown On...
Transportation

Ways to Get Around Town:

On Campus
CMU Shuttle Service
6:30 a.m.-6:30 p.m.
(412) 268-7433

CMU Escort
6:30 p.m.-2:30 a.m., after 2:30 a.m. by request
(412) 268-2323

Public Transportation
Port Authority Transit (PAT)
(412) 442-2000
Pick up bus schedules from the University Center Information Desk.

Taxi Cabs
People's Cab Co.
(412) 681-3131

Yellow Cab Co.
(412) 665-8100

Car Rentals

Alamo
(412) 472-5060
(800) 327-9633
http://www.alamo.com

Avis
(412) 472-5200
(800) 831-2847
http://www.avis.com

Budget
(412) 472-5252
(800) 527-0700
http://www.budget.com

Dollar
(412) 472-5100
(800) 800-4000
http://www.dollar.com

Enterprise
(412) 472-3490
(800) 736-8222
http://www.enterprise.com

Hertz
(412) 472-5955
(800) 654-3131
http://www.hertz.com

National
(412) 472-5094
(800) 227-7368
http://www.nationalcar.com

Best Ways to Get Around Town:

• Weasel a friend into a ride
• Pittsburgh City Buses—they are free, just bring your ID
• A bike
• A mean set of sneakers

How To Get Out of Pittsburgh:

Airlines Serving Pittsburgh:

American Airlines
(800) 433-7300
www.americanairlines.com

Continental
(800) 523-3273
www.continental.com

Delta
(800) 221-1212
www.delta-air.com

Northwest
(800) 225-2525
www.nwa.com

Southwest
(800) 435-9792
www.southwest.com

TWA
(800) 221-2000
www.twa.com

United
(800) 241-6522
www.united.com

US Airways
(800) 428-4322
www.usairways.com

Airport:
Pittsburgh International Airport
(412) 472-3525

The Pittsburgh International Airport is 22 miles and approximately 30 minutes driving time from Carnegie Mellon.

How to Get to the Airport:
Airlines Transportation Company Inc.
(412) 471-8900

Airport Flyer
Port Authority Transit's 28X Airport Shuttle
(412) 442-2000.

The bus stops in front of Carnegie Mellon, and the trip takes about forty minutes. Free with student ID.

Cab
A Cab Ride to the Airport Costs: $35

Greyhound
Pittsburgh Greyhound Trailways Bus Terminal
(4 miles from campus)
11th Street & Liberty Ave.
Pittsburgh, PA 15222
(412) 392-6513
(800) 231-2222.
www.greyhound.com

Amtrak
Pittsburgh Amtrak Train Station
(4 miles from campus)
1100 Liberty Ave.
Pittsburgh, PA 15222
(412) 471-6172
(800) 872-7245.
www.amtrak.com

Travel Agents
Council Travel
118 Meyran Avenue, Oakland
(412) 683-1881

Forbes Travel
5835 Forbes Avenue, Sq. Hill
(412) 521-7300

World-Wise Travel
3039 West Liberty Avenue
(412) 531-5555

Students Speak Out On...
Transportation

{ **"I feel like the transportation situation is pretty good. You can't really get from neighborhood to neighborhood, though. The transportation system only gets you around within different neighborhoods."**

Q "All CMU students get a sticker on their ID card that allows them to **ride the bus for free.** You can get anywhere you want on the buses and they come pretty often."

Q "**The buses are really great!** You can go just about any-where via bus. You get a free Pittsburgh bus pass with your $36,000 tuition! That's really nice of them! A fun game to play on a Sunday is 'how far can you get in the city via the buses?' Try it sometime if you don't have work, but that'll never hap-pen."

Q "Public transportation is real spotty. The buses go most any-where, but you never know what time they'll show up or how often. Pittsburgh is cutting back on their public transportation services soon as well, so it will not be as easy to get around. **Meet your feet**—your new favorite form of public transpor-tation."

Q "**Buses are awesome and free with your student ID,** so you can get anywhere in Pittsburgh and the surrounding neighborhoods."

Q "Public transportation—mainly the bus system—is great be-cause **it goes everywhere and is free!** If you ever need to fly anywhere, the airport here is one of the best in the country! You can even catch a bus to and from the airport for free."

Q "Public transportation is great. **It's better than the shuttle bus that the campus provides.** You can ride as many times as you'd like as long as you have your ID."

Q "**You can't catch a cab by flagging them down**, but you can call them up and hope they'll arrive on time. Buses are easy to catch during the day. I say get a car, a fast one!"

Q "It can take you where you need to go; **you just need to know the schedule.** And you pay for it as part of your student fees, anyway, so you might as well use it.."

Q "I'm very impressed with the bus system. If you know the right buses, **you can really get around.**"

Q "It's very convenient. CMU gives you stickers for access to the buses and as many rides as you can think of. **Buses are a pain sometimes because they're often late**, but there are no major problems. You can get basically anywhere with them with some patience."

Q "**Pittsburgh transportation sucks.** The buses are always late and the way you pay is ridiculous. It's either 'pay enter' or 'pay leave.' I think it depends on what the driver wants, so it's a bit confusing."

Q "The bus system **takes you everywhere**—the mall, the suburbs, the airport, downtown—and there are several bus stops on campus."

The College Prowler Take On...
Transportation

Public transportation is the only way to travel for most students. Every student gets free access to the bus system, and most students take full advantage of this. Pittsburgh, as a city, is spread out among a number of distant areas. To get to most out of these places you'll need to take the bus, especially since driving can get a little confusing. Though it sometimes can be a pain to wait fifty minutes for a bus that doesn't seem like it's ever going to come, off-campus life would be crippled without the bus system.

It only takes a few weeks to learn the bus system, and once you've familiarized yourself with it, you're golden. Your CMU bus pass is your key to exploring all areas of the city. The PAT buses are some of the cleanest and safest around.

The College Prowler™ Grade on
Transportation: B+

A high grade for Transportation indicates that campus buses, public buses, cabs and rental cars are readily available and affordable. Other determining factors include proximity to an airport and the necessity of transportation.

Weather

The Lowdown On...
Weather

Average Temperature

Fall: 53 °F
Winter: 30 °F
Spring: 50 °F
Summer: 71 °F

Average Precipitation

Fall: 2.83 in.
Winter: 2.64 in.
Spring: 3.33 in.
Summer: 3.82 in.

Students Speak Out On...
Weather

{ **"The weather is unpredictable at best. It's freezing here right now, and it's the end of May! I like the weather, though, because it always keeps you on your toes. I'd be bored in a place where it never changed."**

Q "I can't stand the weather in Pittsburgh. I mean, there are some beautiful days, but then **some really crappy ones.** There is a lot of rain. We often have overcast skies, and it gets pretty cold. That's one bad thing, oh well! Mother Nature, what can one do?"

Q "Pittsburgh weather is . . . flaky. **It rains a lot in the spring** and fall, and it snows a lot in the winter. The winter can get really cold, so bring your long johns. The late spring is a great time to be on campus, though. The sunshine and warm weather brings students out of their rooms and into the cut for some seriously-needed tanning."

Q **"The weather is freezing, miserable, and inhospitable.** You sometimes feel like God wants you to die in this freezing, hellish wasteland."

Q "It's pretty overcast most of the time. You'll get some sunny days, and you'll get some freezing cold days, but **bring a rain-coat.** If you're from warm weather, you better be prepared for a frigid winter. Bring warm clothes. You'll live in hooded sweat-shirts and comfy pants. People don't dress up for class; people wear whatever they want. Fashion isn't big, academics are."

Q "Weather sucks. It's freezing cold in the winter and blazing hot in the summer. **The seasons are all messed up**—they switch around all the time. It rains so much, and it's overcast most of the time. The bad weather makes Pittsburgh a much more depressing city than it would otherwise be. Then again, what did you expect from a city that sits inside a giant ditch?"

Q "Pittsburgh weather changes a lot! One day it will be 50 degrees, and the next one could have a temperature of 90. **It rains often**, and the winter can be cold and snowy. I like it because it changes so much. One of my classmates is from Hawaii, where it is always 80 degrees and sunny. He loves it that the seasons change! I would say it is not too much different from New York City; we are only about seven hours away."

Q "The weather sucks. **I come from Florida, so I think it's horrid.** It was really hot in the summer, but right now it's beautiful because it's not too hot and it's not really cold. But, once winter hits, its winter. I mean, I have never lived in snow, so I think it sucks, but I can't really compare it to anything. It doesn't snow like eight inches, but it snows sometimes, and it gets kind of cold."

Q "**Weather is strangely unpredictable.** It may seem sunny in the morning, and it may suddenly start snowing in the evening. It may look fine during the day, and it may rain at night all of a sudden. I don't like the weather here at all. That's why I like to stay in my room most of the time."

Q "Most people think of Pittsburgh as a rainy, dreary city; but that is just the stereotype. It's hot in August and September. In October and November, it cools down. It's cold in December and possibly snowy into January. **Spring time is nice and the best time of year in Pittsburgh.**"

The College Prowler Take On...
Weather

In Pittsburgh, the blue sky is often obscured by gray clouds. On clear days, however, the town is like an entirely different place—people are cheery and the school's population almost seems to double. Students often complain about the weather. If the climate was nicer, maybe most students wouldn't always be holed up doing work.

One of the first jokes you'll probably hear about Pittsburgh will be about the weather. It's rare that you'll have a day where the blue sky is not obscured by gray clouds. Rain is a constant year round, and the snow was pretty bad last winter. In the summer, Pittsburgh gets really humid, and everyone does what they can to stay cool. When you come to campus in the fall, wear shorts and a T-shirt, but make sure to pack winter clothes when you first come because the weather gets very cold very fast. Bringing some snow boots wouldn't be a bad idea either.

The College Prowler™ Grade on

Weather: C-

A high Weather grade designates that temperatures are mild and rarely reach extremes, that the campus tends to be sunny rather than rainy, and that weather is fairly consistent rather than unpredictable.

Report Card Summary

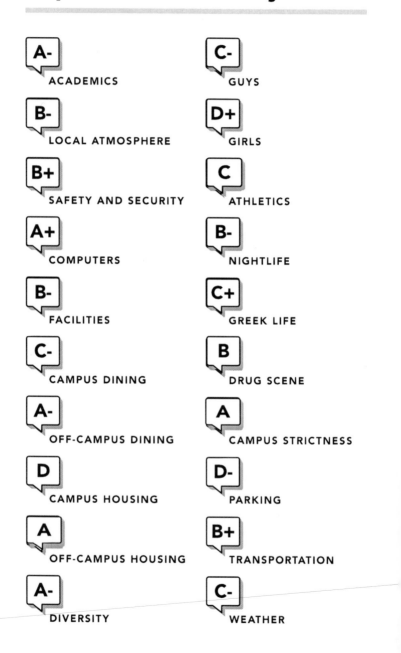

A-
ACADEMICS

C-
GUYS

B-
LOCAL ATMOSPHERE

D+
GIRLS

B+
SAFETY AND SECURITY

C
ATHLETICS

A+
COMPUTERS

B-
NIGHTLIFE

B-
FACILITIES

C+
GREEK LIFE

C-
CAMPUS DINING

B
DRUG SCENE

A-
OFF-CAMPUS DINING

A
CAMPUS STRICTNESS

D
CAMPUS HOUSING

D-
PARKING

A
OFF-CAMPUS HOUSING

B+
TRANSPORTATION

A-
DIVERSITY

C-
WEATHER

Overall Experience

Students Speak Out On...
Overall Experience

{ "I like CMU a lot, but I wish it was in a different location. Pittsburgh weather can get you down sometimes, but luckily, you get twelve free sessions per year with a psychologist."

"I don't wish I was anywhere else. **CMU has a ton of real interesting people**. Students are racially diverse, live diverse lifestyles, and think different thoughts."

"I went to a larger university first and then transferred to CMU. **I like the small, school atmosphere.** You'll never be in a thousand-person lecture, and you'll always be able to get in touch with your professor or a TA. It's the kind of school that if you are ambitious and want to do something, you can do it. From starting a club to bringing a concert or event to campus, CMU is the kind of place that appreciates diversity and unique students and events."

Q "**Pittsburgh grows on you** and then you realize that it is a real cool place. Don't expect it to be like other cities such as New York or Philly because it's not. While those cities have a hot downtown, Pittsburgh, because of its history, doesn't have a great downtown scene but has incredible neighborhoods all over the place. Get to them all and check them out; there is some great stuff going on in there."

Q "**This school is not for everybody.** CMU is a good institution that requires a lot of patience when dealing with the social scene and academic community. People here are weird. The campus is split into many subgroups of interests and studies. Do not believe what the school tells you about interdisciplinary studies. It's a crock! If I had to do it over again, I would go to a state school with a good media arts department. If you were a fairly social person in high school and enjoy going to parties and interacting with interesting and stimulating people, don't come to CMU. If you never took your head out of the books and now want a school that will accept you for being all the dork you can be, welcome home."

Q "I love CMU. Sure, there are minor things that I may dislike from time to time—things that you will find at any school—but after coming here, I cannot imagine going to any other school. This was the school for me because of the intense program. **However, this is not the place for everyone.** It's difficult to come here without having a sense of what you want to study. Everyone here in every academic program is highly focused. I'd say most students are very hard workers and really care. That's why it is such a good place for me; everyone is enthusiastic about their educations. I really think this school is a great place, but you probably won't know for sure until you get here, I surely didn't."

Q "Here's the deal: If you are serious about education and you are serious about getting somewhere, then this place will help you do it. **This is not a big party school.** If you just want to mess around and party and get laid all the time, go somewhere else."

Q "**Job-wise, you can't do better than here**. It's a very good school, and there are a lot of opportunities. I'm not kidding about that; it's a great academic institution, but you have to be serious about it. You will work harder than you've ever worked before. I coasted through high school, but I'm majoring in cognitive science and computer science now, and it kicks my butt. As long as you are prepared to do the work, then you will have a great experience; everything else just sort of falls into place."

Q "It's not my type of place because I'm more of a partier than most people. **I was more popular in high school than most people.** I think a lot of people are into studying, but the fraternity I am in does plenty of partying, so I manage. To be honest, if the school wasn't so good for an education, I would be somewhere else."

Q "It's a lot of work, that's for sure. I would definitely say that we get a lot more work than most Ivy Schools, from what I've heard. If you're at CMU and are majoring in something that we're not known for, then I would definitely go elsewhere. If you're coming here for computers or engineering and maybe business, then it's beneficial and **the opportunities are endless.** I would never change schools for anything. Then again, I'm someone who would be comfortable anywhere. But, if you do come to CMU for any of those majors, be prepared to work your butt off. I believe CMU has a lot of weird people, but that's just because you're surrounded by people who are doing truly amazing things. I'm always impressed by my peers and I'm always proud of my school, but the social thing is not one of our strong points. You can get by, but it's definitely not one of our strengths."

Q "Here's a very important piece of advice: **Do not let first semester get you all worked up.** I think everyone has their troubles adjusting. I was really considering leaving and going somewhere else, but that's not the case anymore. I expected all these things to happen when I got here and they didn't. Why they didn't happen was basically because I was living in a dream world. You just need to get adjusted, and that's the most difficult part. Also, when you're at orientation, be outgoing and meet as many people as you can! It's fun, it's hard, but you'll meet a lot of interesting people; trust me. Overall, I'm glad that I'm at CMU."

Q "I wanted to transfer to NYU for sophomore year, but as the semester went by, I met a lot of people, and they really made my experience at CMU a good one. Another friend wanted to leave initially, but now she absolutely loves it. Honestly, **I really enjoyed my freshman year.**"

Q "I wanted to transfer to Pitt my freshman year because I didn't think I was smart enough and I didn't really fit in with the competitive, nerdy people. That idea ended quickly because I was too lazy to apply to Pitt. I can't see myself being anywhere else now. **You couldn't pay me to go to another school.** I'm practically obsessed with CMU now. You've got to love it for what it is. Tartan pride!"

Q "I can't imagine being anywhere else. I actually just graduated, and I'm sticking around for the summer because I'm not ready to leave. I know I'll be back to visit, as well. I think **the school is so darn cool because of the diversity and its strength in both the arts and sciences.** Not only is it one of the best computer science schools, but it's also one of the best drama schools (not to mention other majors, but those two are such opposites). I can't think of any other highly-ranked school that is so strong in such differing areas of study. CMU students and alumni are everywhere doing important things in their fields—from people like Holly Hunter and Ted Danson to the people that developed the technology for broadcasting the Super Bowl in 360 degrees."

The College Prowler Take On...
Overall Experience

In appraising CMU, most students are appreciative of the fantastic education they're receiving and the one-of-a-kind experience that the campus offers. At CMU, students have an unprecedented opportunity to explore their fields of study. Sometimes it's hard for students to see all opportunities that Carnegie Mellon gives them. Students who are unhappy with their experience are often frustrated with the sub-par social situation or the massive amount of work.

No matter how fed-up students get with the amount of work, the social scene, or the bad weather, students are often glad they came to CMU when they think about the unique experience the school has given them. The academic opportunities you will receive at CMU are astounding and everyone on campus is truly dedicated to learning. Though the time spent at CMU may not fulfill some students' hopes of living a wild youth, the years spent at Carnegie Mellon can be just as exciting in some ways. It's different. And for people who don't want the same college experience as everyone else, it can be exciting.

The Inside Scoop

The Lowdown On...
The Inside Scoop

CMU Slang

Know the slang, know the school. The following is a list of things you really need to know before coming to CMU. The more of these words you know, the better off you'll be.

The UC: The University Center. This is the main student center on campus.

CFA: College of Fine Arts; Can't Fu----n Spell.

H&SS: Humanities & Social Science; High School Studies; Hot, Sexy, & Stupid; H & Less

Stress.

CS: Computer Science; Can't Score, Classes Suck.

The Dungeon: The basement of Donner Hall.

Big Blue: Donner Residence Hall.

The O: The Original Hot Dog Shop.

The Quad: Where the fraternities are located.

Sree's: The Indian guy that sells food out of his minivan.

Moonlight: The Asian food

truck.

Schlag: Hamerschlag Hall; a dorm.

The Fence: Fence in the middle of campus that gets painted by students for tradition.

The Cut: Carnegie Mellon's central lawn.

P.H.I. or PHI BAR: Panther Hollow Inn, a popular bar right off campus.

The Mall: The grassy space between Baker, Hamerschlag, Wean, and Doherty Halls.

The Donner Ditch: An area behind Donner Hall. The site of numerous BBQs.

Flagstaff: A grassy hill behind Hunt Library and Baker Hall; part of Schenley Park.

Maggie Mo: Nickname for Margaret Morrison, a building on campus.

Cluster: A computer lab.

The Old Gym: Skibo Gym.

The New Gym: The workout facility at the University Center.

The Trucks: Food trucks on Tech Street.

The Black Chairs: The black leather chairs in the middle of the UC where people meet; also known as the Airport Lounge.

Cat Man: Cathedral Mansions; campus-leased student housing apartments.

C-Cons: The computer lab assistants.

DA: Desk Attendant.

OLR: Online Registration.

Fingering: A UNIX command to find information on a system user.

The Hub: Enrollment offices in the basement of Warner Hall. Pay your tuition here.

CSW: Computer Skills Workshop.

MINI 1 & MINI 2: One semester can be divided into two mini sessions. A few classes are offered in this shorter format.

MISC. MARKET: An online bulletin board where students post random messages and sell things.

Things I Wish I Knew Before Coming to CMU

- Get on the smallest meal plan possible

- Go to the frats during Orientation Week

- Don't skip "Playfair" during Orientation

- Don't buy the bed sheets and linens from the school catalog

- It's not a big party school

- It's really technical

- How hard the workload is

- How to manage my time better

- It's not a good school for people who are undecided about their majors

Tips to Succeed at CMU

- Pick classes you actually like

- Research your professors before choosing your classes

- Actually go to class

- Don't ever fall behind

- Check your e-mail at least ten times a day

- Do your homework yourself so you actually understand the material

- Ask the TAs tons of questions

- Always dispute bad grades

- Know what you want to study before coming here

CMU Urban Legends

• Bill Gates once offered to hire CMU's whole graduating Computer Science class

• Playboy ranked CMU the 2nd ugliest campus in America

• Endowment at CMU is very small, which is why its ranking doesn't go up

• Wean Hall houses back-up computers for the Department of Defense

• A complete network of steam tunnels provides an underground way to get around the whole campus.

School Spirit

Even if students aren't bursting with school spirit, they're still proud of the Carnegie Mellon name. Because there's an overwhelming lack of popular sports teams and the colleges within the University are fairly segregated, students don't have much to unite and rally around. Engineers, drama students, business majors, and arc-ies (Architecture) all swell with pride for their fields of study. It's not uncommon to see students wearing clothing that bears the CMU logo, but it's rare that students will dress up beyond that. During the popular Carnival Week, when students are racing in buggies and building booths, school spirit is at a yearly high. A fair share of the on-campus population will even express a subdued hatred for the University because of all the work they have to do.

CMU Traditions

Bagpipes
CMU has a strange and storied tradition of bagpipe playing. It's not uncommon to hear the comforting (shrill) noise of the pipes floating through campus on almost any night of the week. This is one of CMU's more eccentric endearing traditions that has come to grow on students. CMU is the only university in the country to offer a degree in bagpipe music.

Lunar Gala
Do you like fashion? Lunar Gala, an annual fashion show run by students, is an extremely popular on-campus event. All clothes are designed, sewn, and modeled by students. Students work very hard to make their creative fashion ideas a reality.

Dancers' Symposium
Dancers' Symposium is held yearly at the end of Fall and Spring semester. The show features student choreographed dances ranging in style from ballet to hip-hop. Any student can volunteer to dance or choreograph a dance. Many students perform in more than one dance.

Clipper Ship
The Clipper Ship is constantly offering leisure boat trips around Pittsburgh's three rivers. During orientation week, CMU reserves an entire ship for the incoming freshmen class to party on all night. Upon graduation, seniors ride the ship again in a trip bidding farewell to CMU. As a freshman, it's a great way to meet new friends. As a senior, it's a fun way to say goodbye to everyone you've gotten to know over your CMU career.

Misc. Market
Misc. Market is the name of an electronic bulletin board run by CMU. Posting to Misc. Market is an addictive and habitual activity for many students. The board has developed its own sub-culture that is a source of pride for many of its patrons. Through Misc. Market, you can buy a lot of useful items from students and locals; you can also get yourself involved in a flame war if you post too many wisecracks to the board.

The Fence
In the middle of The Cut at the center of CMU's campus is The Fence. While The Fence, itself, serves no practical purpose, it's a Carnegie Mellon tradition for students to paint personal messages or advertisements for parties on it. Students can only paint The Fence after midnight, and once it's painted, they must sleep outside to guard it from other students eager to paint it again before sunrise.

The Kiltie Band
Decked out in full Scottish gear and ready to release blaring bagpipe music, CMU's Kiltie Band an 80-plus year tradition is an antiquated but beloved campus tradition. The band has been performing at every home football game since CMU hosted Notre Dame on Andrew Carnegie's birthday in 1922.

Buggy
Buggies are small cylindrical push carts that students race around the campus streets during Carnival Week. The buggies are piloted by a "pusher," and are steered by the driver, a female student who is situated within the buggy. Students prepare all year, building and testing their buggies so that they'll be ready to race in time for Spring Carnival.

The Green Room Wall
A tradition within the College of Fine Arts is for senior drama students to autograph the Green Room's walls and ceilings before graduating. The Green Room is located on campus behind the stage of Kresge Theatre.

Greek Sing
Greek Sing is an annual event where CMU's Greek organizations perform original song and dance routines to support a local charitable organization. Every March, the fraternities and sororities compete to raise money for a good cause and to see which Greek organizations can put on the best show.

Finding a Job or Internship

The Lowdown On...
Finding a Job or Internship

If you are worried about finding a job after going to school, don't feel like you're on your own. CMU Career Center offers a number of services for its students. Just keep in mind that many students still cite networking as one of the best ways to make connections and find a job.

Advice

From the moment you walk on campus, get in touch and stay in contact with the Career Center. Also, make sure to attend the BOC (Business Opportunities Conference), TOC (Technical Opportunities Conference), and TIE (Technical Internship Exposition) these are crucial conferences to attend.

Career Center Resources & Services

- Campus Employment

- Career Counseling

- Placement Advising

- Career Workshops

- The Resource Center

- Graduate School Advising

- TartanTRAK

Career Center Announcement b-board:
cmu.career-center.announce (upcoming events, campus interview postings, job fair announcements)

AVERAGE SALARY INFORMATION

The Lowdown:

The following statistics represent average starting salaries for CMU graduates by major. If the information for a specific major does not exist, it means that fewer than four students have reported salary offers.

Carnegie Institute of Technology

Chemical Engineering	$54,333
Civil & Environmental Engineering	$38,714
Electrical & Computer Engineering	$56,189
Material Sciences & Engineering	$49,575
Mechanical Engineering	$51,686

College of Fine Arts

Information Not Available

Mellon College of Science

Biology	$38,967
Chemistry	$57,510
Mathematics	$53,369
Physics	$53,795
Social & Decision Sciences	$43,427

Humanities and Social Sciences

Economics	$54,750
English	$43,444
Psychology	$35,774
Information Systems	$55,000

School of Industrial Administration

Computing & Information Technology	$53,007
Finance	$51,913
General Management	$51,800
Manufacturing, Management & Consulting	$52,667
Marketing	$43,900
Overall	$53,493

School of Computer Science

Computer Science	$61,695

Alumni

The Lowdown On...
Alumni

Website:
http://www.cmu.edu/alumni

Email:
Alumni-house@andrew.cmu.
edu

Office:
Alumni House
5017 Forbes Ave
Pittsburgh, PA 15213
(800) 2-CMU-ALUM

Services Available
Lifetime e-mail forwarding

➜

The Alumni House:
The Alumni House is right across the street from the UC and has meeting rooms, a small kitchen, and a friendly staff. It is open 8:30 a.m.-5 p.m. on weekdays during the regular school year. The office of alumni relations supports the 60,000 member Carnegie Mellon Alumni Association.

Major Alumni Events
The biggest events for alumni are Homecoming, Spring Carnival, and Class Reunions. Homecoming takes place in October and features a football game; Spring Carnival is in April and features buggy and booth; and class reunions take place year-round and can be found on the alumni website.

Alumni Publications
Carnegie Mellon Magazine

CMU Magazine comes out four times a year and engages 81,000 readers to keep them up-to-speed with CMU life. Yearly subscriptions are $8.

Did You Know?

Famous CMU Alums

Rob Marshall (Class of '82), Academy Award winning director/choreographer

Andy Warhol (Class of '49), founded the '60s Pop art movement, Died in 1987

Ted Danson (Class of '72), star of TV Show "Cheers"

Holly Hunter (Class of '80), star of movie "The Piano"

Ming-Na Wen (Class of '86), voice of Mulan and actress in the Joy Luck Club and ER

John Wells (Class of '66), creator and producer of TV Shows "Hill Street Blues," "LA Law," and "NYPD Blue"

Vinod Khosla (Class of '78), former CEO of Sun Microsystems and leading Silicon Valley venture capitalist

Student Organizations

Activities Board - www.andrew.cmu.edu/org/AB

Aikido - www.andrew.cmu.edu/org/aikido/

ALLIES - an organization for people of all sexual orientations coming together to support gays, lesbians, and bisexuals. www.andrew.cmu.edu/allies

Amnesty International - Carnegie Mellon Chapter www.andrew.cmu.edu/org/amnesty-int

Asian Student Association (ASA)

Association for India's Development (AID) - www.andrew.cmu.edu/~aid

Association for Industrial Management and Economics (AIME) - www.andrew.cmu.edu/~aime/

Astronomy Club - www.contrib.andrew.cmu.edu/~astroc

Bagpipe Band - www.andrew.cmu.edu/~pipeband/

Ballroom Dance Club - www.contrib.andrew.cmu.edu/~ballroom

Black Graduate Student Organization (BGSO) - www.andrew. cmu.edu/org/BGSO

Bridge Club - www.andrew.cmu.edu/~dr4b/bridge-club.html

Carnegie Threads - www.contrib.andrew.cmu.edu/~quilt/home. html   Quilting Club

Christians on Campus

CMU College Republicans - www.andrew.cmu.edu/~cmucr

CMU Masters Swimming Club

cmuOUT - a group of lesbian, gay, and bisexual members of the campus community, and their friends. www.andrew.cmu.edu/~out

Cycling Club - www.andrew.cmu.edu/~cycling

Dancer's Symposium - www.andrew.cmu.edu/org/dancer/ DANCERSYMPOSIUM.html

Doctors of Carnegie

Earth - www.andrew.cmu.edu/org/earth/ CMU's environmental club.

East End Tutoring Program - outreach.mac.cc.cmu.edu/EEYP/ EastEnd.html

Eclectic Studies Group - www.contrib.andrew.cmu.edu/ ~eclectic/

Emergency Medical Service (CMU EMS) www.andrew.cmu. edu/~cmu/ems

Eta Kappa Nu - the International Honor Society for Electrical Engineers. www.ece.cmu.edu/~hkn/

Explorers Club – an outdoor activities club. www.andrew.cmu.edu/org/explorers

Fiesta – organizes a campus-wide celebration, in honor of the past academic year and in anticipation of summer. www.andrew.cmu.edu/~fiesta/

Filmmaking@cmu www.andrew.cmu.edu/proj/film/

Fringe - promotes a spirit of friendship. www.andrew.

Hong Kong Students' - Association www.andrew.cmu.edu/org/hksa

Ice Hockey Club - www.andrew.cmu.edu/user/hockey/index.html

Joyful Noise - a Christian a cappella singing group. www.andrew.cmu.edu/~jn

KGB www.contrib.andrew.cmu.edu/org/kgb

Mayur - an Indian Student Organization. www.contrib.andrew.cmu.edu/~mm3m/

Muslim Students Association of CMU - www.andrew.cmu.edu/~msa

Oakland Review - Carnegie Mellon University's annual literary-arts journal. english.cmu.edu/or

CMU Origami Club - www.contrib.andrew.cmu.edu/org/origami/home.html

Pi Delta Psi Fraternity, Inc.

Persian Student Organization (PSO)

PIONEERS - www.andrew.cmu.edu/user/pioneers/

Carnegie Tech Radio Club (W3VC) - www.contrib.andrew.cmu.edu/~ar99/

Russian House - www.andrew.cmu.edu/org/RussianHouse/

SALSA - a Latin and Hispanic culture club

Scotch'n'Soda Theater -Carnegie Mellon's student-run theater company. www.andrew.cmu.edu/~sns/

Society of Hispanic Professional Engineers (SHPE)

Society of Physics Students

Society of Women Engineers - www.andrew.cmu.edu/org/swe

SPIC MACAY - Society for the Promotion of Indian Classical Music and Culture Amongst Youth. www.contrib.andrew.cmu.edu:8001/org/macay/home

Carnegie Mellon Speech & Parliamentary Debate Society www.andrew.cmu.edu/org/debate

Spring Carnival - www.andrew.cmu.edu/org/carnival/

String Ensemble

Students for the Exploration and Development of Space - only international space organization run entirely by students. www.andrew.cmu.edu/user/seds/

Students in Free Enterprise

Student Pugwash

Student Senate - www.andrew.cmu.edu/user/ss2p/

Student Union - Carnegie Mellon's alternative news journal

Taiwanese Students Association - www.andrew.cmu.edu/~tsa

Tau Beta Pi, Pennsylvania Gamma chapter - www.cit.cmu.edu/taubetapi

WRCT 88.3 fm - Carnegie Mellon's student-run radio station. www.wrct.org/

The Best &
The Worst

The Ten **BEST** Things About CMU:

1 Carnival

2 Diversity

3 Plays at the Purnell Center

4 Painting The Fence at midnight

5 The $1 movies in the UC

6 Flirting through e-mail & Instant Messenger

7 Chillin' on The Cut on a nice day

8 PHI on Thursday nights

9 Restaurants with late-night, half-price food

10 Bagpipes

The Ten **WORST** Things About CMU:

1 Bagpipes

2 Finding a parking spot

3 Meal plan/dining

4 Sporadic weather

5 The Hub

6 Teachers with heavy accents

7 The Smell of the Old Student Center

8 Skibo Gym

9 Introverts

10 Boy/girl ratio

Visiting CMU

The Lowdown On...
Visiting CMU

HOTEL INFORMATION

Shadyside:

Appletree Bed and Breakfast
http://www.appletreeb-b.com/
703 S. Negley Ave.
Pittsburgh, PA 15232
(412) 661-0631
Distance from Campus: Less than a mile
Price Range: $140-$190

Friendship Suites
http://www.friendshipsuites.com/
301 Stratford Ave.
Pittsburgh, PA 15232
(412) 392-1935
Distance from Campus: 1.5 miles
Price Range: $79-$119

Shadyside Inn
http://www.shadysideinn.com/introduction.html

5405 Fifth Ave.
Pittsburgh, PA 15232
(412) 682-2300
Distance from Campus: Less than a mile
Price Range: $99-$139

Sunnyledge

5124 Fifth Ave.
Pittsburgh, PA 15232
(412) 683-5014
Distance from Campus: Less than a mile
Price Range: $139-$275

Oakland:

Best Western - University Center

http://www.bestwestern.com/
3401 Boulevard of the Allies
Pittsburgh, PA 15213
(412) 683-6100
(800) 245-4444
Distance from Campus: 1.4 miles
Price Range: $85

Hampton Inn

http://www.pittsburghhamptoninn.com/
3315 Hamlet Street
Pittsburgh, PA 15213
(412) 681-1000
(800) HAMPTON
Distance from Campus: 1.4 miles
Price Range: $89-$119

Holiday Inn Select - University Center

http://www.basshotels.com/holiday-inn
100 Lytton Ave.
Pittsburgh, PA 15213
(412) 682-6200
(800) 864-8287
Distance from Campus: Less than a mile
Price Range: $123-$144

Residence Inn by Marriott

http://www.residenceinn.com/
3896 Bigelow Blvd.
Pittsburgh, PA 15213
(412) 621-2200
(800) 331-3131
Distance from Campus: 1 mile
Price Range: $139-$189

University Club

123 University Pl.
Pittsburgh, PA 15213
(412) 621-1890
Distance from Campus: Less than 1 mile
Price Range: $99-$109

Wyndham Garden Hotel - University Place

http://www.wyndham.com/
3454 Forbes Ave.
Pittsburgh, PA 15213
(412) 683-2040
(877) 662-6242
Distance from Campus: 1 mile
Price Range: $89-$129

Downtown:

Hilton Towers
http://www.hilton.com/
600 Commonwealth Pl.
Pittsburgh, PA 15222
(412) 391-4600
Distance from Campus: 4.2 miles
Price Range: $189-$219

Morning Glory Inn Bed and Breakfast
http://www.morningglo-rybedandbreakfast.com/
2119 Sarah St.
Pittsburgh, PA 15203
(412) 431-1707
Distance from Campus: 3 miles
Price Range: $150-$190

Omni William Penn
http://www.starwood.com/wes-tin/index.html
530 William Penn Pl.
Pittsburgh, PA 15219
(412) 281-7100
Distance from Campus: 4 miles
Price Range: $116-$159

Pittsburgh Marriott City Center
http://www.marriott.com/pitdt
112 Washington Pl.
Pittsburgh, PA 15219
412-471-4000
1-888-456-6600
Distance from Campus: 5 miles
Price Range: $99-$159

Renaissance Pittsburgh Hotel
http://www.renaissancehotels.com/
107 Sixth St.
Pittsburgh, PA 15222
412-562-1200
1-866-454-4400
Distance from Campus: 3 miles
Price Range: $129-$169

Sheraton Hotel-Station Square
http://www.usahotelguide.com/states/pennsylvania/pittsburgh/sheraton.html
Station Square Dr.
Pittsburgh, PA 15219
(412) 261-2000
(800) 255-7488
Distance from Campus: 4.2 miles
Price Range: $79-$119

Westin Convention Center Pittsburgh
http://www.starwood.com/westin/index.html
1000 Penn Ave.
Pittsburgh, PA 15222
(412) 281-3700
(800) 367-8478
Distance from Campus: 4 miles
Price Range: $89-$225

Take a Campus Virtual Tour

http://www.cmu.edu/vrtour

Campus Tours

Campus tours run most Mondays through Fridays (except on holidays, between semesters, during finals and during spring break). Tours depart at 9:30 a.m., 11:30 a.m., 1:30 p.m. and 3:30 p.m. Call in advance of your visit to check the availability of the tour!

To Schedule a Group Information Session or Interview:

Call (412) 268-2082 on any weekday from 8:30 a.m.-5 p.m. Eastern Time.

The admission staff interviews most Mondays through Fridays throughout the year; however, because of the time involved in reviewing applications, no interviews will be conducted from January 1 through May 1.

Sleeping Bag Weekend:

Wanna live the life of a CMU student for a day and a half? CollegeProwler strongly recommends visiting CMU during a Sleeping Bag Weekend. Expect to receive an invitation from CMU if you are on their mailing list. If you are not on their mailing list, call (412) 268-2082 or e-mail cmsbw@andrew.cmu. edu During Sleeping Bag Weekend, you'll be able to meet other CMU students, faculty, deans, admissions officers, so bring this book with you and grill everyone you can with questions!

IMPORTANT TIP: Remember, Sleeping Bag Weekend might be the greatest time of your life, but even 1.5 days at CMU might not give you an accurate portrayal of campus.

PROWL AROUND! Go find some students at the UC that are just hanging out. Most students at CMU can be very helpful if you take the initiative to introduce yourself and nicely ask them for help.

Directions to Campus

Driving from the North/West

Take the Pennsylvania Turnpike east to Exit 28, Perry Highway. Follow Interstate 79 South to 279 South (Exit 72). Follow signs and go over the Fort Duquesne Bridge. Take 376 East to Exit 2A, Forbes Avenue/Oakland. Stay in the right-hand lanes, following Forbes 1.3 miles through the Oakland business district to campus. Immediately at the intersection of Forbes Avenue and Beeler Street, turn right into the parking garage on campus.

Driving from the South

Take Interstate 79 North to 279 North (Pittsburgh). Follow 279 North toward Pittsburgh through the Fort Pitt Tunnel and onto the Fort Pitt Bridge. Once on the bridge, stay in the far right lanes and follow signs for 376 East/Monroeville. Take 376 East to Exit 2A, Forbes Avenue/Oakland. Stay in the right-hand lanes, following Forbes 1.3 miles through the Oakland business district to campus. Immediately at the intersection of Forbes Avenue and Beeler Street, turn right into the parking garage on campus.

Driving from the East

Take the Pennsylvania Turnpike West to Exit 57, Pittsburgh/ Monroeville. Follow Interstate 376 West to Exit 7, Edgewood/ Swissvale. Turn right onto Braddock Avenue (at the end of the ramp). Continue to the Forbes Avenue inter-section. (Frick Park will be on the left). Turn left onto Forbes Avenue and follow Forbes Avenue approximately three miles to campus. Immediately at the intersection of Forbes Avenue and Beeler Street, turn left into the parking garage on campus.

Words to Know

Academic Probation – A student can receive this if they fail to keep up with their school's academic minimums. Those who are unable to improve their grades after receiving this warning can possibly face dismissal.

Beer Pong / Beirut – A drinking game with numerous cups of beer arranged in a particular pattern on each side of a table. The goal is to get a ping pong ball into one of the opponent's cups by throwing the ball or hitting it with a paddle. If the ball lands in a cup, the opponent is required to drink the beer.

Bid – An invitation from a fraternity or sorority to pledge their specific house.

Blue Light Phone – Brightly-colored phone posts with a blue light bulb on top. These phones exist for security purposes and are located at various outside locations around most campuses. If a student has an emergency or is feeling endangered, they can pick up one of these phones (free of charge) to connect with campus police or an escort service.

Campus Police – Policemen who are specifically assigned to a given institution. Campus police are not regular city officers; they are employed by the university in a full-time capacity.

Club Sports – A level of sports that falls somewhere between varsity and intramural. If a student is unable to commit to a varsity team but has a lot of passion for athletics, a club sport could be a better, less intense option. If a club sport still requires too much commitment, intramurals often involve no traveling and a lot less time.

Cocaine – An illegal drug. Also known as "coke" or "blow," cocaine often resembles a white crystalline or powdery substance. It is highly addictive and dangerous.

Common Application – An application that students can use to apply to multiple schools.

Course Registration – The time when a student selects what courses they would like for the upcoming quarter or semester. Prior to registration, it is best to have an idea of several back-up courses in case a particular class becomes full. If a course is full, a student can place themselves on the waitlist, although this still does not guarantee entry.

Division Athletics – Athletics range from Division I to Division III. Division IA is the most competitive, while Division III is considered to be the least competitive.

Dorm – Short for dormitory, a dorm is an on-campus housing facility. Dorms can provide a range of options from suite-style rooms to more communal options that include shared bathrooms. Most first-year students live in dorms. Some upperclassmen who wish to stay on campus also choose this option.

Early Action – A way to apply to a school and get an early acceptance response without a binding commitment. This is a system that is becoming less and less available.

Early Decision – An option that students should use only if they are positive that a place is their dream school. If a student applies to a school using the early decision option and is admitted, they are required and bound to attend that university. Admission rates are usually higher with early decision students because the school knows that a student is making them their first choice.

Ecstasy – An illegal drug. Also known as "e" or "x," ecstasy looks like a pill and most resembles an aspirin." Considered a party drug, ecstasy is very dangerous and can be deadly.

Ethernet – An extremely fast internet connection that is usually available in most university-owned residence halls. To use an Ethernet connection properly, a student will need a network card and cable for their computer.

Fake ID – A counterfeit identification card that contains false information. Most commonly, students get fake IDs and change their birthdates so that they appear to be older than 21 (of legal drinking age). Even though it is illegal, many college students have fake IDs in hopes of purchasing alcohol or getting into bars.

Frosh – Slang for "freshmen."

Hazing – Initiation rituals that must be completed for membership into some fraternities or sororities. Numerous universities have outlawed hazing due to its degrading or dangerous requirements.

Sports (IMs) – A popular, and usually free, student activity where students create teams and compete against other groups for fun. These sports vary in competitiveness and can include a range of activities—everything from billiards to water polo. IM sports are a great way to meet people with similar interests.

Keg – Officially called a half barrel, a keg contains roughly 200 12-ounce servings of beer and is often found at college parties.

LSD – An illegal drug. Also known as acid, this hallucinogenic drug most commonly resembles a tab of paper.

Marijuana – An illegal drug. Also known as weed or pot; besides alcohol, marijuana is one of the most commonly-found drugs on campuses across the country.

Major –The focal point of a student's college studies; a specific topic that is studied for a degree. Examples of majors include physics, English, history, computer science, economics, business, and music. Many students decide on a specific major before arriving on campus, while others are simply "undecided" and figure it out later. Those who are extremely interested in two areas can also choose to double major.

Meal Block – The equivalent of one meal. Students on a "meal plan" usually receive a fixed number of meals per week.

Each meal, or "block," can be redeemed at the school's dining facilities in place of cash. More often than not, if a student fails to use their weekly allotment of meal blocks, they will be forfeited.

Minor – An additional focal point in a student's education. Often serving as a compliment or addition to a student's main area of focus, a minor has fewer requirements and prerequisites to fulfill than a major. Minors are not required for graduation from most schools; however some students who want to further explore many different interests choose to have both a major and a minor.

Mushrooms – An illegal drug. Also known as "shrooms," this drug looks like regular mushrooms but are extremely hallucinogenic.

Off-Campus Housing – Housing from a particular landlord or rental group that is not affiliated with the university. Depending on the college, off-campus housing can range from extremely popular to non-existent. Those students who choose to live off campus are typically given more freedom, but they also have to deal with things such as possible subletting scenarios, furniture, and bills. In addition to these factors, rental prices and distance often affect a student's decision to move off campus.

Office Hours – Time that teachers set aside for students who have questions about the coursework. Office hours are a good place for students to go over any problems and to show interest in the subject material.

Pledging – The time after a student has gone through rush, received a bid, and has chosen a particular fraternity or sorority they would like to join. Pledging usually lasts anywhere from one to two semesters. Once the pledging period is complete and a particular student has done everything that is required to become a member, they are considered a brother or sister. If a fraternity or a sorority would decide to "haze" a group of students, these initiation rituals would take place during the pledging period.

Private Institution – A school that does not use taxpayers dollars to help subsidize education costs. Private schools typically cost more than public schools and are usually smaller.

Prof – Slang for "professor."

Public Institution – A school that uses taxpayers dollars to help subsidize education costs. Public schools are often a good value for in-state residents and tend to be larger than most private colleges.

Quarter System (sometimes referred to as the Trimester System) – A type of academic calendar system. In this setup, students take classes for three academic periods. The first quarter usually starts in late September or early October and concludes right before Christmas. The second quarter usually starts around early to mid–January and finishes up around March or April. The last quarter, or "third quarter," usually starts in late March or early April and finishes up in late May or Mid-June. The fourth quarter is summer. The major difference between the quarter system and semester system is that students take more courses but with less coverage.

RA (Resident Assistant) – A student leader who is assigned to a particular floor in a dormitory in order to help to the other students who live there. A RA's duties include ensuring student safety and providing guidance or assistance wherever possible.

Recitation – An extension of a specific course; a "review" session of sorts. Because some classes are so large, recitations offer a setting with fewer students where students can ask questions and get help from professors or TAs in a more personalized environment. As a result, it is common for most large lecture classes to be supplemented with recitations.

Rolling Admissions – A form of admissions. Most commonly found at public institutions, schools with this type of policy continue to accept students throughout the year until their class sizes are met. For example, some schools begin accepting students as early as December and will continue to do so until April or May.

Room and Board – This is typically the combined cost of a university-owned room and a meal plan.

Room Draw/Housing Lottery – A common way to pick on-campus room assignments for the following year. If a student decides to remain in university-owned housing, they are assigned a unique number that, along with seniority, is used to choose their new rooms for the next year.

Rush – The period in which students can meet the brothers and sisters of a particular chapter and find out if a given fraternity or sorority is right for them. Rushing a fraternity or a sorority is not a requirement at any school. The goal of rush is to give students who are serious about pledging a feel for what to expect.

Semester System – The most common type of academic calendar system at college campuses. This setup typically includes two semesters in a given school year. The "fall" semester starts around the end of August or early September and finishes right before winter vacation. The "spring" semester usually starts in mid-January and ends around late April or May.

Student Center/Rec Center/Student Union – A common area on campus that often contains study areas, recreation facilities, and eateries. This building is often a good place to meet up with fellow students and is most commonly used as a hangout. Depending on the school, the student center can have a huge role or a non-existent role in campus life.

Student ID – A university-issued photo ID that serves as a student's key to many different functions within an institution. Some schools require students to show these cards in order to get into dorms, libraries, cafeterias, and other facilities. In addition to storing meal plan information, in some cases, a student ID can actually work as a debit card and allow students to purchase things from bookstores or local shops.

Suite – A type of dorm room. Unlike other places that have communal bathrooms that are shared by the entire floor, a suite has a private bathroom. Suite-style dorm rooms can house anywhere from two to ten students.

TA (Teacher's Assistant) – An undergraduate or grad student who helps in some manner with a specific course. In some cases, a TA will teach a class, assist a professor, grade assignments, or conduct office hours.

Undergraduate – A student who is in the process of studying for their Bachelor (college) degree.

ABOUT THE AUTHOR:

I had a great time writing this book! I've been looking for a chance to express myself through my writing, and the entire experience has been very exciting. I'm hoping to publish more in the future as I continue to grow as a writer. I'm now a junior at Carnegie Mellon tirelessly pursuing degrees in both Professional Writing and Business Administration. In the future I hope to utilize the skills I've learned in both of my majors. Pittsburgh is the first place I've lived since leaving my native Northern New Jersey. Coming to college here it's been a dizzying and maturing experience to say the least. I hope this book has been insightful for you, and I hope you had a few laughs while reading it. If you have any questions or comments please contact me by e-mail at DanielLieberman@collegepro wler.com.

Here's where my biography takes a turn from overly narcissistic self commentary. I'd like to give many people many thanks. Thank you Mom, Dad, Amanda, Grandpa, Ragonesi's, Kobus-kie's, Liebermann's, Becky, CheeChee, Tom, Aaron, Drew, Jer-emy, Meredith, Red Beavis, Rose, Mr. Gaul, Horatio Flatbush, Honus, Jason, Jen, Johnson, Keara, Nick, Scott, and everyone at College Prowler!

Daniel Liebermann
DanielLieberman@collegeprowler.com.

Tell Us What Life Is Really Like At Your School!

Have you ever wanted to let people know what your school is really like? Now's your chance to help millions of high school students choose the right school.

Let your voice be heard and win cash and prizes!

Check out **www.collegeprowler.com** for more info!

Notes

Do You Have What It Takes To Get Admitted?

The College Prowler Road to College Counseling Program is here. An admissions officer will review your candidacy at the school of your choice and create a 12+ page personal admission plan. We rate your credentials with the same criteria used by school admissions committees. We assess your strengths and weaknesses and create a plan of action that makes a difference.

Check out **www.collegeprowler.com** or call 1.800.290.2682 for complete details.

Notes

Pros and Cons

Still can't figure out if this is the right school for you?
You've already read through this in-depth guide; why not
list the pros and cons? It will really help with narrowing down
your decision and determining whether or not
this school is right for you.

Pros	Cons

Notes

....

....

....

....

....

....

....

....

....

....

....

....

....

....

Need Help Paying For School?

Apply for our Scholarship!

College Prowler awards thousands of dollars a year
to students who compose the best essays.
E-mail *scholarship@collegeprowler.com* for more
information, or call 1.800.290.2682.

Apply now at **www.collegeprowler.com**

Notes

....

....

....

....

....

....

....

....

....

....

....

....

....

....

Get Paid To Rep Your City!

Make money for college!

Earn cash by telling your friends about College Prowler!

Excellent Pay + Incentives + Bonuses

Compete with reps across the nation for cash bonuses

Gain marketing and communication skills

Build your resume and gain work experience for future career opportunities

Flexible work hours; make your own schedule

Opportunities for advancement

Contact *sales@collegeprowler.com*
Apply now at **www.collegeprowler.com**

Notes

....

....

....

....

....

....

....

....

....

....

....

....

....

Do You Own
A Website?

Would you like to be an affiliate of one of the
fastest-growing companies in the publishing industry?
Our web affiliates generate a significant income
based on customers whom they refer to our
website. Start making some cash now! Contact
sales@collegeprowler.com for more information
or call 1.800.290.2682

Apply now at **www.collegeprowler.com**

Notes

....

....

....

....

....

....

....

....

....

....

....

....

....

....

Notes

Write For Us!
Get Published! Voice Your Opinion.

Writing a College Prowler guidebook is both fun and rewarding; our open-ended format allows your own creativity free reign. Our writers have been featured in national newspapers and have seen their names in bookstores across the country. Now is your chance to break into the publishing industry with one of the country's fastest-growing publishers!

Apply now at **www.collegeprowler.com**

Contact *editor@collegeprowler.com* or call 1.800.290.2682 for more details.

Notes

....

....

....

....

....

....

....

....

....

....

....

....

....

....

Notes

....
....
....
....
....
....
....
....
....
....
....
....
....